W9-BLW-224

BIOLOGY
SUCCESS
In 20 Minutes a Day

DATE DUE

FEB 2 6 2009	
SEP 3 0 2009	
SEP 1 5 2013	

BRODART, CO.   Cat. No. 23-221

BIOLOGY
SUCCESS
In 20 Minutes
a Day

Mark Kalk

LEARNINGEXPRESS®

NEW YORK

Copyright © 2005 LearningExpress, LLC.

All rights reserved under International and Pan-American Copyright Conventions.
Published in the United States by LearningExpress, LLC, New York.

Library of Congress Cataloging-in-Publication Data:
Kalk, Mark.
   Biology success in 20 minutes a day / Mark Kalk.
      p. cm.
    ISBN 1-57685-483-3
   1. Biology—Study and teaching. I. Title. II. Title: Biology success in twenty minutes a day.
QH315.K29 2005
570—dc22   2005001796

Printed in the United States of America

9 8 7 6 5 4 3 2 1

ISBN 1-57685-483-3

For more information on LearningExpress, other LearningExpress products, or bulk sales, please write to us at:
   LearningExpress
   55 Broadway
   8th Floor
   New York, NY 10006

Or visit us at:
   www.learnatest.com

LIBRARY SERVICES
AUSTIN, TX

Contents ▶

Introduction

If you have never taken a biology course and now find that you need to know biology, this is the book for you. If you have already taken a biology course but felt like you never understood what the teacher was trying to tell you, this book can teach you what you need to know. If it has been a while since you have taken a biology course, and you need to refresh your skills, this book will review the basics and reteach you the skills you may have forgotten. Whatever your reason for needing to know biology, *Biology Success* will teach you what you need to know. It gives you biology basics in clear and straightforward lessons that you can do at your own pace.

How to Use This Book

Biology Success teaches basic biology concepts in 20 self-paced lessons. The book includes a pretest, a posttest, tips on how to prepare for a standardized test, and an appendix of additional resources for further study. Before you begin Lesson 1, take the pretest. The pretest will assess your current biology abilities. You'll find the answer key at the end of the pretest. Each answer includes the lesson number that the problem is testing. This will be helpful in determining your strengths and weaknesses. After taking the pretest, move on to Lesson 1.

Each lesson offers detailed explanations of a new concept. Numerous examples are presented with step-by-step solutions. As you proceed through a lesson, you will find tips and shortcuts that will help you learn a concept. A practice set of problems follows each new concept. The answers to the practice problems are in an answer key located after a set of practice questions.

When you have completed all 20 lessons, take the posttest at the end of the book. The posttest has the same format as the pretest, but the questions are different. Compare the results of the posttest with the results of the pretest you took before you began Lesson 1. What are your strengths? Do you have weak areas? Do you need to spend more time on some concepts, or are you ready to go to the next level?

Make a Commitment

Success does not come without effort. If you truly want to be successful, make a commitment to spend the time you need to improve your biology skills. Once you achieve biology success, you have laid the foundation for future challenges and opportunities.

So sharpen your pencil, and get ready to begin the pretest!

BIOLOGY
SUCCESS
In 20 Minutes a Day

▶ Pretest

Before you begin Lesson 1, you may want to get an idea of what you know and what you need to learn. The pretest will answer some of these questions for you. The pretest is 35 multiple-choice questions covering this book's topics. Although 35 questions can't cover every concept, skill, or shortcut taught in this book, your performance on the pretest will give you a good indication of your strengths and weaknesses. Keep in mind the pretest does not test all the skills taught in this book.

If you score high on the pretest, you have a good foundation and should be able to work your way through the book quickly. If you score low on the pretest, don't despair. This book will take you through the biology concepts step by step. If you get a low score, you may need to take more than 20 minutes a day to work through a lesson. However, this is a self-paced program, so you can spend as much time on a lesson as you need. You decide when you fully comprehend the lesson and are ready to go on to the next one.

Take as much time as you need to do the pretest. When you are finished, check your answers with the answer key at the end of the chapter. Along with each answer is the lesson that covers the algebra skills needed for that question. You will find that the level of difficulty increases as you work your way through the pretest. Use the following grid to record your answers.

1. ⓐ ⓑ ⓒ ⓓ	13. ⓐ ⓑ ⓒ ⓓ	25. ⓐ ⓑ ⓒ ⓓ
2. ⓐ ⓑ ⓒ ⓓ	14. ⓐ ⓑ ⓒ ⓓ	26. ⓐ ⓑ ⓒ ⓓ
3. ⓐ ⓑ ⓒ ⓓ	15. ⓐ ⓑ ⓒ ⓓ	27. ⓐ ⓑ ⓒ ⓓ
4. ⓐ ⓑ ⓒ ⓓ	16. ⓐ ⓑ ⓒ ⓓ	28. ⓐ ⓑ ⓒ ⓓ
5. ⓐ ⓑ ⓒ ⓓ	17. ⓐ ⓑ ⓒ ⓓ	29. ⓐ ⓑ ⓒ ⓓ
6. ⓐ ⓑ ⓒ ⓓ	18. ⓐ ⓑ ⓒ ⓓ	30. ⓐ ⓑ ⓒ ⓓ
7. ⓐ ⓑ ⓒ ⓓ	19. ⓐ ⓑ ⓒ ⓓ	31. ⓐ ⓑ ⓒ ⓓ
8. ⓐ ⓑ ⓒ ⓓ	20. ⓐ ⓑ ⓒ ⓓ	32. ⓐ ⓑ ⓒ ⓓ
9. ⓐ ⓑ ⓒ ⓓ	21. ⓐ ⓑ ⓒ ⓓ	33. ⓐ ⓑ ⓒ ⓓ
10. ⓐ ⓑ ⓒ ⓓ	22. ⓐ ⓑ ⓒ ⓓ	34. ⓐ ⓑ ⓒ ⓓ
11. ⓐ ⓑ ⓒ ⓓ	23. ⓐ ⓑ ⓒ ⓓ	35. ⓐ ⓑ ⓒ ⓓ
12. ⓐ ⓑ ⓒ ⓓ	24. ⓐ ⓑ ⓒ ⓓ	

1. What is the substance called that fills a cell inside its cell membrane?
   a. metabolic fluid
   b. cytoplasm
   c. nucleoplasm
   d. lipoproteins

2. In which of the following organisms would cells have a cell wall?
   a. dog
   b. human
   c. grass
   d. fish

3. Metabolism refers to
   a. uncontrolled division of cancer cells.
   b. irregularity in the shape of a cell.
   c. transformation of a normal cell into a cancer cell.
   d. the biochemical reactions that support life.

4. Sometimes, an allele on one chromosome will suppress the phenotypic expression of an allele on its paired chromosome. This is an example of
   a. dominance.
   b. meiosis.
   c. carrier recognition.
   d. consanguinity.

5. The process of respiration includes
   a. resting and digesting.
   b. inhalation and gas exchange.
   c. circulatory constriction.
   d. synaptic conduction.

6. Nitrogen fixation, whereby atmospheric, gaseous nitrogen is assimilated into chemical compounds, is a process performed by which organism?
   a. plants
   b. animals
   c. fungi
   d. bacteria

7. The orientation of a plant toward or away from light is called
   a. photogenesis.
   b. phototropism.
   c. photosynthesis.
   d. photoautotrophism.

8. The major sites of photosynthesis in most plants are the
   a. stems.
   b. seeds.
   c. leaves.
   d. roots.

9. The cellular component or organelle where photosynthesis takes place is the
   a. chloroplast.
   b. mitochondrion.
   c. Golgi body.
   d. nucleus.

10. Angiosperms are different from gymnosperms because
    a. they produce flowers.
    b. they have seeds.
    c. they reproduce only asexually.
    d. they are limited in their growth rate.

11. With relation to the idea of survival of the fittest, which of the following is the best measure of the fittest organism?
   a. physical strength
   b. reproductive success
   c. winning a combat for resources
   d. winning a combat for a mate

12. A distinguishing feature of the Kingdom Monera is that the cells of the organisms in that Kingdom
   a. contain many organelles.
   b. contain mitochondria.
   c. obtain food through photosynthesis.
   d. do not have a nucleus.

13. Which of the following categories of classification is the least specific?
   a. phylum
   b. class
   c. order
   d. genus

14. Which of the following characteristics best distinguishes nonliving organisms from living organisms?
   a. Nonliving organisms can change position.
   b. Nonliving organisms can reproduce.
   c. Nonliving organisms are complexly organized.
   d. Nonliving organisms are stationary.

15. The nephron is part of which of the following organs?
   a. brain
   b. intestine
   c. kidney
   d. heart

16. Which of the following is known as the "powerhouse of the cell"?
   a. chloroplast
   b. vacuole
   c. endoplasmic reticulum
   d. mitochondrion

17. Which of the following structures is part of a plant cell but not of an animal cell?
   a. mitochondrion
   b. ribosome
   c. chloroplast
   d. endoplasmic reticulum

18. Which of the following statements is true?
   a. Cells form organs, which form tissues, which form systems.
   b. Cells form tissues, which form organs, which form systems.
   c. Tissues form cells, which form organs, which form systems.
   d. Systems form cells, which form tissues, which form organs.

19. The principal function of blood platelets is to
   a. help clot blood.
   b. carry oxygen.
   c. produce antibodies.
   d. consume bacteria.

20. The two or more related genes that control a trait are known as
   a. chromosomes.
   b. chromatids.
   c. phenotypes.
   d. alleles.

21. Which of the following is an example of natural selection?
  a. the development of flies that were resistant to the chemical DDT after it became widely used to kill household pests
  b. an increase in the average yearly egg production by chickens who were selected by breeders because of their high egg production
  c. an inherited characteristic, such as long necks in giraffes, that is passed on and occurs generation after generation
  d. the development of penicillin and other antibiotics for the treatment of bacterial infections

22. Which of the following is NOT a member of the Fungi Kingdom?
  a. mushroom
  b. yeast
  c. mold
  d. algae

23. Which of the following is a characteristic function of the Plant Kingdom?
  a. photosynthesis
  b. respiration
  c. digestion
  d. inhalation

24. Which of the following organs functions to absorb water and create feces from undigested food?
  a. small intestine
  b. liver
  c. large intestine
  d. stomach

25. In vertebrate animals, muscles consist mainly of which tissue?
  a. epithelial
  b. cardiac muscle
  c. smooth muscle
  d. striated muscle

26. What is the light-sensitive pigment found in green plants?
  a. cytochrome
  b. melanin
  c. chlorophyll
  d. hemoglobin

27. The position a plant or animal occupies in the food chain may also be referred to as its
  a. productivity.
  b. producer level.
  c. biomass.
  d. trophic level.

28. Water and nutrients move through transport tubes, such as xylem and phloem, in which of the following plant groups?
  a. nonvascular plants
  b. tracheophytes
  c. mosses
  d. liverworts

29. What is the process in which genetic information contained in the DNA molecule is transferred to a messenger RNA molecule?
  a. transduction
  b. transcription
  c. translation
  d. mitosis

30. The flowers of a flowering plant are part of which generation?
   a. second
   b. sporophyte
   c. first
   d. gametophyte

31. In vertebrate animals, which of the following are cell fragments that play a key role in blood clotting?
   a. platelets
   b. neutrophils
   c. red blood cells
   d. monocytes

32. According to the binomial classification system, which of the following categories is the most specific (or has the smallest number of organisms)?
   a. phylum
   b. genus
   c. class
   d. order

33. Which of the following is the main function of the urinary bladder?
   a. to convert urea to urine
   b. to absorb water
   c. to store urine for excretion
   d. to store bile salts

34. Blood from the lungs travels to the left atrium of the heart through the
   a. aorta.
   b. vena cava.
   c. pulmonary artery.
   d. pulmonary vein.

35. Muscles perform which of the following operations?
   a. contraction and expansion
   b. contraction only
   c. expansion only
   d. neither contraction nor expansion

▶ Answers

If you miss any of the answers, you can find help for that kind of question in the lesson shown to the right of the answer.

1. b. Lesson 10

2. c. Lesson 5

3. d. Lesson 11

4. a. Lesson 19

5. b. Lesson 14

6. d. Lesson 4

7. b. Lesson 17

8. c. Lesson 5

9. a. Lesson 10

10. a. Lesson 5

11. b. Lesson 20

12. d. Lesson 3

13. a. Lesson 3

14. d. Lesson 2

15. a. Lesson 17

16. d. Lesson 10

17. c. Lesson 10

18. b. Lesson 10

19. a. Lesson 15

20. d. Lesson 19

21. a. Lesson 20

22. d. Lesson 3

23. a. Lesson 5

24. c. Lesson 11

25. d. Lesson 13

26. c. Lesson 5

27. d. Lesson 7

28. b. Lesson 5

29. b. Lesson 19

30. d. Lesson 18

31. a. Lesson 15

32. b. Lesson 3

33. c. Lesson 16

34. d. Lesson 15

35. b. Lesson 13

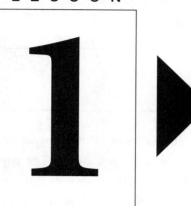
Living and Nonliving Matter and the Chemicals of Life

Most of us naturally sort objects around us into *living* (animate) beings or *nonliving* (inanimate) objects. However, sometimes it is hard to tell the difference or we may have to stretch our definitions of living versus nonliving. This lesson looks at some of the principles of chemistry underlying living systems.

▶ Atoms and Elements

Living organisms and inanimate objects are all composed of atoms. The way in which atoms are arranged into more complex molecules and how those molecules interact determines whether something is alive or not. Around one hundred elements can be found on Earth and in the rest of the universe. If you divide any element into its smallest part, you will have what we call an *atom*. An *element* is made up of one and only one type of atom (although trillions of these same atoms exist in even a tiny piece of the element).

Elements are arranged according to the number of *protons* they have in their nucleus. Thus, hydrogen, with only one proton, is the first element. The number of *electrons* equals the number of protons. Electrons are exchanged and shared in chemical reactions, but protons remain untouched during such reactions. The *neutrons* in the *nucleus* also remain untouched. The number of neutrons varies and, along with the protons, contributes to the mass of the atom. The electrons are so small that their mass is not included in the mass of the whole atom.

An atom is composed of even smaller particles called *protons*, *neutrons*, and *electrons*. These particles are common to all atoms. The number of these particles will determine the uniqueness of an atom and thus an element.

The neutrons and protons are combined in the center of the atom, a region called the *nucleus*. The electrons are located in cloud-like layers where they spin around the nucleus.

Electron Shells

The electrons in atoms concentrate into layers surrounding the nucleus. These layers are called *shells*. Each atom needs to fill out the number of electrons in each of its shells. Atoms with complete shells are "content" and do not easily participate in chemical reactions. Chemical reactions occur when electrons are shared or transferred between atoms. Atoms that do not have complete electron shells tend to be more reactive and participate in chemical reactions.

Atoms can complete their electron shells in one of two ways. They can acquire them through a transfer, or they can share them with other atoms. When two or more atoms combine, we call the resulting compound a *molecule*.

Ionic Bonds

When electrons are transferred between atoms, each becomes an *ion* with either a positive or negative electric charge. The opposite charges then attract each ion to the other. Sodium and chlorine form ions that are attracted to each other in a molecule called sodium chloride, otherwise known as table salt. Bonds between ions are called *ionic bonds*.

Covalent Bonds

When atoms share electrons, they are said to have formed a *covalent bond*. A good example of a molecule with covalent bonding is water. Water consists of one oxygen atom and two hydrogen atoms. The oxygen atom needs two electrons to complete its outer shell, and each hydrogen atom needs one electron. The oxygen atom can thus form a covalent bond with each of the two hydrogen atoms.

Chemical Bonds and Energy

Most atoms are joined with others to form molecules. These molecules, in turn, can combine to form larger molecules and new substances. Living organisms take simple molecules and combine them into complex chemical substances. However, life also breaks down complex molecules as a way of acquiring energy. All the bonds in a molecule contain energy, and when large molecules are broken down by living systems, this bond energy is released. It is this bond energy that sustains living systems. Living organisms use this energy to grow and develop. They are in a constant state of change yet remain essentially the same. This is called a *dynamic equilibrium* because change is always occurring, but the organism remains what it is intended to be. This continues until the organism dies, when it will be decomposed into simpler molecules. This process is in contrast to inorganic, nonliving molecules like *minerals*. Minerals may undergo change, but they do not grow and develop.

The Most Common Elements in Living Matter

- Oxygen
- Carbon
- Hydrogen
- Nitrogen
- Calcium
- Phosphorous
- Chlorine

- Sulfur
- Potassium
- Sodium
- Magnesium
- Iodine
- Iron

► Molecules of Life

The molecules of life are most commonly made from a dozen or so elements. Because they very often contain carbon, they are also referred to as *organic molecules*. The most important biological molecules are lipids, proteins, carbohydrates, and nucleic acids.

Lipids are also called fats and are substances that act as an energy reserve and as a protective cushion for vital organs. Sometimes, lipids will combine with other molecules to form important compounds. The membranes around cells are composed of molecules called *phospholipids*. Hormones like estrogen and testosterone are lipid-type molecules also known as *steroids*. Cholesterol is also a lipid-type molecule.

Proteins are complex molecules and represent about half of the dry weight of an animal's body. Proteins are made from a series of smaller molecules called *amino acids*. Proteins have two very valuable functions in living organisms. They form structures like muscles, bones, and other organs, and they are specialized molecules called *enzymes*. Enzymes are molecules that facilitate chemical reactions to make them more efficient. The enzymes are not used up in the chemical reaction and are not part of the final product.

Carbohydrates are made up of only carbon, hydrogen, and oxygen. Carbohydrate molecules provide energy (though less than lipid molecules) and structural components of organisms (especially plants). The main type of carbohydrates is *sugars*, which provide abundant and quick energy for all cells. Brain cells are exclusively dependent upon a constant source of sugar molecules. Starch-type carbohydrates are more complex than sugars and are not soluble in water; thus, they act as a longer-term storage depot of energy. In animals, this storage carbohydrate is called *glycogen* and is somewhat different in composition than the starch found in plants. *Cellulose* is a special carbohydrate found in plants, and it is primarily responsible for the structural support of plants. Because the many plants in the world have so much cellulose, it is one of the most abundant organic molecules on Earth.

Nucleic acids are large molecules made up of smaller molecules called *nucleotides*. The most familiar example of nucleic acids is the DNA molecule. DNA is *deoxyribonucleic acid* and is responsible for carrying and transmitting genetic information. Thus, nucleic acids are responsible for two of the hallmark characteristics of life: reproduction and evolution.

▶ Practice

1. Molecules consist of
   a. only protons and neutrons.
   b. only electrons and neutrons.
   c. whole atoms.
   d. bonds of energy.

2. An ionic bond is formed when two atoms
   a. share electrons.
   b. transfer electrons.
   c. share protons.
   d. transfer protons.

3. Water has covalent bonds because the oxygen and hydrogen atoms
   a. share electrons.
   b. transfer electrons.
   c. share protons.
   d. transfer protons.

4. Life depends upon
   a. the bond energy in molecules.
   b. the energy of protons.
   c. the energy of electrons.
   d. the energy of neutrons.

5. Which of the following elements is NOT found in carbohydrates?
   a. carbon
   b. hydrogen
   c. oxygen
   d. sulfur

6. Which of the following are carbohydrate molecules that provide quick energy for cells, especially brain cells?
   a. amino acids
   b. glycogen
   c. sugars
   d. lipids

▶ Answers

1. c. Molecules are combinations of whole atoms, not just protons, neutrons, or electrons. Bonds of energy are what keep the atoms in place to form the molecules.

2. b. Ionic bonds form when two atoms have transferred electrons and thus acquire opposite electrical charges. These opposite electrical charges attract the ions to each other to form a bond and thus a molecule.

3. a. Covalent bonds refer to the fact that the atoms in the molecule share electrons to complete each other's electron shells.

4. a. Living organisms use the energy contained in bonds to fuel all life processes.

5. d. All the other elements listed are exactly what make up a carbohydrate molecule. Sulfur is usually found in proteins.

6. c. Sugars are a simple carbohydrate that can be utilized quickly to provide energy for cells. Glycogen is a more complex carbohydrate, and it takes longer for it to be broken down for energy. Lipids and amino acids are not carbohydrates (although both can be used for energy if carbohydrate energy is not available).

▶ In Short

Living organisms are made up of many molecules, some complex and others relatively simple. Molecules are made of atoms. Atoms are made from protons and neutrons in a centrally located nucleus, surrounded by layers or shells of electrons. The important molecules of life are lipids, proteins, carbohydrates, and nucleic acids.

2 ▶ What Is Life?

We seem to have an intuitive sense of how to answer the question, "what is life?" Most of us can distinguish between something that is living versus something that is not living (or was once living but is now dead). We can sometimes be fooled, but most of the time, we get it right. This lesson will summarize the qualities of life that distinguish it from inanimate objects or those things that were once living.

▶ Life Performs Actions

One general way to view living things is to notice that they carry out functions and undergo changes, often self-directed. A rock may undergo changes during erosion, and it may even move in a stream or during an earthquake. However, none of these changes or movements is self-directed. The rock is passive and things happen to it.

A living organism moves when it needs to and performs a full range of other functions, some at a visible level (such as movement or eating) and others at a smaller, less visible scale (such as the chemical reactions of digestion or the changes in a neuron during nerve signal transmission). So in this sense, the level of complexity indicates whether something is living or not.

Characteristics of Living Things

In general, living things are different from inanimate objects because they can perform self-directed functions and actions, are structurally and functionally complex, are able to reproduce, are able to respond to the environment, and can evolve.

Life Has Levels of Complexity

A television set or a computer may seem complicated, but each really consists of only a few chemical elements and a few dozen parts. Rocks, for example, are made of one or a few chemical elements. However, simple, one-celled microorganisms such as a bacterium are made of dozens of chemical elements and molecules. These molecules are built up into thousands of more complex molecules and form dozens of structures.

Larger, multicelled plants or animals (like ourselves) have a dizzying array of molecules and interrelated parts. Living things are based on cells, the smallest unit of life. These cells are grouped together to form *tissues*, as, for example, millions of liver cells grouped together form liver tissue. Different tissues are grouped together to form an organ, so liver tissue, blood tissue, and connective tissue all combine to form the organ we call the liver. Many organs will be grouped together to form organ systems. Using the liver example, we can group it with the intestines, the pancreas, and the stomach to form what we call the digestive system. This layering of ever-increasing complexity is a hallmark characteristic of life.

Life Reproduces Itself

Inanimate objects can last for a very long time and even appear to be indestructible. Living things don't last forever; they wear out or die. However, life continues because organisms can reproduce. New organisms (offspring) are produced when the original organisms (parents) reproduce. Though the parents will die, their offspring will produce even more offspring to continue life.

Even if you break a rock in half, you don't really have more rock, just two pieces instead of one. And the rock doesn't decide to break itself; the action is not

CHARACTERISTIC	LIVING ORGANISM	NONLIVING OBJECT
Can perform actions and functions	Yes, continually	No, or not self-directed
Level of complexity	High, layered	Low
Reproduction	Yes	No
Reaction to stimulus	Yes, actively interacts with environment	No, except simple changes of position or chemical composition
Evolution	Yes	No, except simple chemical changes

self-directed as it is in the reproduction of living organisms. Thus, another indicator of life is the ability to reproduce.

Life Reacts to Environmental Stimuli

Living organisms are irritable; they can take notice of a disturbance. When the environment provides a stimulus, an organism can react to it. Environmental stimuli can be changes in temperature, light, moisture, or many other variables. Inanimate matter such as a rock totally lacks the ability to do this. At best, a rock undergoes some simple change of position (when a strong water current moves it), or it undergoes simple changes in chemical composition (when it crumbles during freezing and thawing).

Animals continually respond to stimuli by moving, migrating to a different place for a whole season, running, hiding, seeking or building shelter, and in thousands of other ways. Irritability or the ability to react to an environmental stimulus is thus another hallmark characteristic that differentiates life from nonlife.

Life Evolves

An organism's ability to respond to its environment can be very valuable. Organisms that are good at doing this will be more likely to survive and reproduce more offspring. When such successful organisms reproduce, they will pass their characteristics on to their offspring. These offspring will also survive well. Organisms that don't react well to their surroundings will most likely die and not reproduce as often. As this slow process continues for a long time, we will see changes in whole populations of organisms. This change over time will result in the evolution of new populations. The process of evolution is thus another distinct characteristic of living beings. Inanimate objects do not engage in this survival of the fittest type of evolution.

▶ Practice

1. The evolution of organisms depends upon their ability to survive and become _____ to their environment, thus being able to produce more offspring.
   a. adapted
   b. accustomed
   c. accommodated
   d. accomplished

2. Irritability refers to an organism's ability to
   a. reproduce.
   b. respond to environmental stimuli.
   c. adapt to its environment.
   d. grow and develop.

3. A nonliving rock has a relatively simple organization. However, living organisms
   a. are even simpler.
   b. are able to reproduce more slowly.
   c. have a layered and complex organization.
   d. move less than rocks.

4. Life continues on because organisms are able to
   a. grow and develop.
   b. move.
   c. react to environmental stimuli.
   d. reproduce.

5. Which of the following is an inanimate object able to do?
   a. evolve through natural selection
   b. warm up by being in the sunlight
   c. reproduce through binary fission
   d. have self-guided movement

▶ Answers

1. a. Adaptation to the external environment is something successful organisms do. As organisms adapt, they may evolve into new organisms over long periods of time. Adapted organisms are able to reproduce more successfully and leave more offspring.

2. b. Irritability means that an organism has receptors that detect a change in the environment. Most organisms then respond to that stimulus by taking some action.

3. c. Living organisms have a complex and layered organization. Nonliving things are more simply constructed.

4. d. Each individual organism is not immortal and will die. However, life itself continues on because organisms reproduce themselves continually.

5. b. Being warmed by the sun is a passive process that happens to both living and nonliving things. Inanimate objects cannot evolve, reproduce, or have self-guided movement as suggested in the other answers.

▶ In Short

Several characteristics distinguish living organisms from nonliving objects. Several such characteristics are grouped into the following categories:

- Life performs actions, often self-directed.
- Life has layers of complexity and is not simple in its structure or function.
- Life reproduces itself.
- Life reacts to environmental stimuli.
- Life evolves.

3 ▶ The Five Kingdoms and Classifying Organisms

Life began as very simple molecules that were bound by membranes. Eventually, these membrane-bound molecules were assembled into more complex structures we call cells. These cells evolved into many forms and even became multicelled collections, leading to organisms such as ourselves. All these organisms adapted to their environment and have characteristics that distinguish them from each other. Scientists have developed systems to organize and classify all of Earth's organisms.

▶ Kingdoms

Life first appeared on Earth as very simple, very tiny microorganisms. These creatures were mostly groups of organic molecules surrounded by a membrane. However, they could feed themselves in some fashion and were able to grow and reproduce. Gradually, over time and through the process of evolution, organisms assumed new forms. Eventually, life on Earth developed into many diverse forms and formed complex relationships. We have been able to organize life into five large groupings called *Kingdoms*. Each Kingdom contains organisms that share significant characteristics that distinguish them from organisms in the other Kingdoms. The five Kingdoms are Animals, Plants, Fungi, Protists, and Bacteria.

The Animal Kingdom

The organisms classified into this Kingdom are multicellular and, because they do not have chlorophyll, are unable to photosynthesize. We call them *heterotrophs*, meaning "eater of others," because they must eat pre-existing organic matter (either plants or other animals) to sustain themselves. Animals have tissues that are more complexly constructed than plants and one-celled organisms. Animals also possess nervous tissue, which has reached high stages of development into nervous systems and brains. Animals are able to move from place to place (locomote) using their muscular systems. We usually divide the Animal Kingdom into two large groups, the vertebrates (animals with backbones) and the invertebrates (animals without backbones).

The Plant Kingdom

Plants are multicellular organisms that use chlorophyll in specialized cellular structures called *chloroplasts* to capture sunlight energy and convert it into organic matter. We refer to plants as *autotrophs* (self-feeders). Also included in the Plant Kingdom are algae that are not multicellular, but are cells with a nucleus (unlike bacteria).

Besides the algae, most plants are divided into one of two groups, the *nonvascular plants* (such as mosses) and the *vascular plants* (such as most crops, trees, and flowering plants). Vascular plants have specialized tissue that allows them to transport water and nutrients from their roots to their leaves and back again, even when the plant is several hundred feet tall. Nonvascular plants cannot do this and remain very small in size. Vascular plants are able to inhabit moist as well as dry environments, whereas nonvascular plants are mostly found in moist, marshy areas because they have no vascular tissue to transport water.

The Fungi Kingdom

Organisms in this Kingdom share some similarities with plants yet maintain other characteristics that make them more animal-like. They lack chlorophyll and cannot perform photosynthesis, so they don't produce their own food and are called *heterotrophs*. However, they reproduce by spores like plants do. They also resemble plants in appearance. The most common representative organisms in this Kingdom are mushrooms, yeasts, and molds. Fungi are very common and are a major benefit to other organisms, including humans. The bodies of fungi are made of filaments called *hyphae*. In large fungi, the hyphae interconnect to form tissue called *mycelium*. The largest organism in the world is believed to be a soil fungus whose mycelium tissue extends for many acres.

The Protist Kingdom

This Kingdom includes single-celled organisms that contain a nucleus as part of their structure. They are a relatively simple cell, but still contain many structures and perform many functions. This Kingdom includes organisms such as paramecium, euglena, amoeba, and slime molds. They often move around using *cilia* or *flagellums*.

KINGDOM	SINGLE OR MULTICELLED	CONTAINS A NUCLEUS	PERFORMS PHOTOSYNTHESIS
Animal	Multicelled	Yes	No, heterotrophic
Plant	Multicelled	Yes	Yes, autotrophic
Fungi	Single and multicelled	Yes	No, heterotrophic
Protist	Single celled	Yes	Both, auto- and heterotrophic
Moneran	Single celled	No	Both, auto- and heterotrophic

The Moneran Kingdom

This Kingdom contains bacteria. All these organisms are single celled and do not contain a nucleus. They have only one chromosome for carrying genetic information, although sometimes they also transmit genetic information using small structures called *plasmids*. They also use flagella to move, like the protists, but their flagella has a different and simpler structure than the protists. They usually reproduce asexually. The bacteria *E. coli (Escherichia coli)* is a member of this Kingdom.

▶ Levels of Classification

A grouping as large as a Kingdom is not very specific and contains organisms defined by broad characteristics. Other levels of classification become gradually more specific until we define an actual specific organism. To classify organisms, we generally start out by grouping them into the appropriate Kingdom. Within each Kingdom, we further subdivide organisms into other groupings. As an example, let's take the wolf:

Kingdom: Animal

Phylum: Chordates (This means the wolf had a notochord that developed into its backbone.)

Class: Mammals (This means the wolf has hair, bears live young, and nurses them with mammary glands.)

Order: Carnivores (This means the wolf is a meat eater.)

Family: *Canids* (This means the wolf has nonretractable claws, a long muzzle, and separate toes.)

Genus: *Canis* (This means the wolf is a member of the dog family.)

Species: *lupus* (This refers to a particular type of wolf known as the European wolf.)

The previous categories form the most common scheme for classifying organisms, although other groupings and other categories are often used. The reason for developing a classifying system is so that we have consistency in how we refer to an organism. If we didn't have this system, then the European wolf described previously would be called wolf in English, *lobo* in Spanish, and *loup* in French. This leads to confusion and a loss of scientific accuracy.

▶ Binomial Nomenclature

The system illustrated here is based on a system developed by Carlos Linneaus. It is called *binomial nomenclature* because in this system, any organism can be positively identified by two Latin words. The other words used previously illustrate where the named organism fits into the whole scheme, but it is only the last two, the Genus and species words, that specifically name an organism. The Genus name is always capitalized and written in italics, whereas the species name is written lowercase but also in italics. Thus, the European wolf is *Canis lupus*, *Canis familiaris* is the common dog, *Felis tigrina* is a tiger, *Felis domesticus* is a common cat, and humans are *Homo sapiens*.

How to Remember the Classification Scheme

Here is an easy way to remember the terms used in this classification scheme:

Kings Play Cards On Friday, Generally Speaking.

If you take the first letter of each word in the sentence and apply it to the proper term in the classification scheme, you will get the following:

Kingdom, Phylum, Class, Order, Family, Genus, Species

► **Practice**

1. A feature that distinguishes organisms from the Kingdom Monera is that their cells
   a. contain specialized organelles.
   b. contain a nucleus.
   c. contain chloroplasts.
   d. lack a nucleus.

2. Which of the following statements is true about the binomial nomenclature system of classification?
   a. The genus and species names describe a specific organism.
   b. The category of Kingdom is very specific.
   c. The category of species is very broad.
   d. Three names are needed to correctly specify a particular organism.

3. Which Kingdom contains organisms that have plant-like and animal-like characteristics?
   a. Animal Kingdom
   b. Plant Kingdom
   c. Fungi Kingdom
   d. Moneran Kingdom

4. Which of the following answers has the different classification levels in the correct order from most general to most specific?
   a. Kingdom, Phylum, Class, Order, Family, *Genus, species*
   b. Order, Family, *Genus, species*, Class, Phylum, Kingdom
   c. *species, Genus*, Family, Order, Class, Phylum, Kingdom
   d. Kingdom, Phylum, Class, *species, Genus*, Family, Order

5. Which of the following Kingdom's members are multicellular AND autotrophic?
   a. Fungi
   b. Animal
   c. Protist
   d. Plant

6. Which of the following Kingdom's members have tissue called mycelium?
   a. Fungi
   b. Animal
   c. Protist
   d. Plant

▶ Answers

1. d. The Monerans (bacteria) lack a nucleus (they are prokaryotes), and their DNA is free floating in the cytoplasm; all other organisms under the classification scheme presented here have a true nucleus (they are eukaryotes).

2. a. In binomial nomenclature, the Genus and species names taken together name a specific and particular organism (humans are *Homo sapiens* and dogs are *Canis familiaris*). Kingdom is a very broad category and species is very specific. It only takes two names to correctly identify a specific organism (the Genus and species).

3. c. The Fungi exhibit characteristics of both the Animal and Plant Kingdoms. The Protist Kingdom also has members that could meet this requirement (such as Euglena), but it is not one of the answer choices.

4. a. This is the correct order from most general (Kingdom) to most specific (species).

5. d. Only plants are multicellular and capable of autotrophism (photosynthesis). The other Kingdoms listed are either not multicellular or not autotrophic.

6. a. Fungi form collections of the root-like hyphae into a tissue called mycelium. The members of the other Kingdoms do not form mycelium tissue.

▶ In Short

Biologists classify organisms based on shared characteristics among groups. The largest level of groupings is the Kingdoms, which consist of Animal, Plant, Fungi, Protist, and Moneran. The Kingdoms are further subdivided into Phylum, Class, Order, Family, Genus, and species. The Genus and species designations form a two-name system, called binomial nomenclature, that specifically identifies a particular organism (for example, humans are designated *Homo sapiens*).

4 ▶ Microorganisms

Microorganisms (microbes) are very small, and most of them cannot be seen with the unaided eye, requiring the use of a microscope or at least a magnifying lens. We can also detect microorganisms by chemical tests. These living beings are everywhere, even in extreme environments such as very hot springs, very cold and dry areas, and even deep in the ocean under tremendous pressure. Some of these organisms cause diseases in animals, plants, and humans; however, most are beneficial to us and the Earth's ecosystems. In fact, we are utterly dependent upon microbes for our quality of life. This lesson will discuss three types of microorganisms: bacteria, protists, and fungi.

▶ Bacteria

Bacteria are microorganisms that do not have a true nucleus; their genetic material is free floating within the cell. Bacteria are very small one-celled organisms and do not contain very complex cell structures. Generally, bacteria come in three varieties: *bacilli* (rod-shaped), *cocci* (sphere-shaped), and *spirilla* (spiral-shaped). Bacteria are prevalent in all environments and are important members of an ecosystem. They are responsible for the breakdown of dead organic matter into its constituent molecules. For this reason, we call bacteria decomposers. They also can be eaten by other organisms and are thus valuable in food-chain relationships. Since bacteria are small, can divide asexually very rapidly, can live practically anywhere, and have great metabolic versatility, they are the most numerous organisms on Earth. Many bacteria, when placed in good conditions, can reproduce every 20 or 30 minutes, each doubling its population after each reproduction.

Benefits of Bacteria

To illustrate the importance of bacteria, let's look at the cycling of the element nitrogen that is used by organisms to make proteins. We will start with dead plants that are being decomposed by bacteria. The nitrogen from the plant tissue is released into the atmosphere, and nitrifying bacteria converts that nitrogen into ammonia-type compounds. Other bacteria act upon these compounds to form nitrates that plants absorb. When these new plants die, we are back again at the decomposing bacteria that release the plant's nitrogen back into the atmosphere.

Bacteria are even in our intestinal tracts to aid in the digestion of food and the manufacturing of vitamins. We derive many benefits from bacteria, but they can also cause us to suffer with diseases.

Bacterial Diseases

Microorganisms, including bacteria, cause many diseases. These organisms enter our bodies in a variety of ways, including airborne transmission, ingestion by mouth, or through the skin when it is cut or injured. We can eliminate this threat by disinfecting utensils and hands or even by the sterilization of objects (the application of high-pressure steam heat). All these methods destroy bacteria and other microorganisms that may cause disease.

▶ Protists

This group is composed of single-celled organisms that have their genetic material contained within a nucleus and have some specialized structures within their cells. These organisms are considered to be more primitive than other organisms with cellular nuclei, but they are more evolved than bacteria (Kingdom Monera). This is a diverse Kingdom consisting of organisms with varied structures and functions, such as amoeba and para-

mecium. Some of this Kingdom's members are autotrophic and contain chlorophyll, whereas others are heterotrophic and must eat other organisms. It is believed that early protists were both animal- and plant-like because they were able to obtain food in both ways. Today, a protist called Euglena does this. Protists are important parts of food chains and ecosystems, and some protists cause disease.

▶ Fungi

The Kingdom Fungi contains single-celled organisms that are heterotrophic in the sense that they do not contain chlorophyll and cannot photosynthesize. Other fungi are multicellular and not microorganisms but function in much the same way as the microscopic forms. However, it is more accurate to describe the ability of multicellular fungi to obtain food in three ways. Saprophytic fungi consume dead organic matter, parasitic fungi attack living plants and animals, and mycorrhizal-associated fungi form close relationships with trees, shrubs, and other plants, where each partner in the relationship mutually benefits.

Fungi produce spores that are very resistant to temperature and moisture extremes. These spores can travel to new areas, thus spreading the fungi organism. The spores can survive for a long time, even in inhospitable environments. When conditions change and become more favorable, the spores germinate and grow. Food is absorbed through structures called *hyphae*. A large mass of interconnected, branching hyphae is called the *mycelium,* which constitutes the main body of the multicellular fungi. However, the mycelium is usually not seen because it is hidden throughout the food source being consumed.

What is most often visible is the fungal fruiting body. A mushroom is a fruiting body that contains the spores. The main body of the mushroom (the mycelium) is under the soil surface. An organism called *lichen* is a mutually beneficial union of a fungus and an algae. Because fungi consume dead organic matter, they play an important decomposition role in an ecosystem. Their actions return nutrients to the soil for eventual uptake by plants.

▶ Practice

1. Fungi consume dead organic matter and thus play an important role in an ecosystem by
   a. making nutrients available for recycling back into the soil.
   b. producing oxygen by photosynthesizing.
   c. producing oxygen by respiration.
   d. living in mostly aquatic environments.

2. Just in numbers alone (but not necessarily mass), which microorganism is the most numerous organism on Earth?
   a. paramecium from the Protist Kingdom
   b. yeast from the Fungi Kingdom
   c. euglena from the Protist Kingdom
   d. bacteria from the Moneran Kingdom

3. Which Kingdom contains organisms that are able to produce nitrates from the nitrogen in the air?
   a. Animal
   b. Plant
   c. Moneran
   d. Protist

4. Why do members of the Fungi Kingdom produce spores?
   a. They are resistant to environmental conditions.
   b. They contain special enzymes.
   c. They are able to photosynthesize.
   d. They are part of the support system.

5. Which of the following is true about the protist euglena?
   a. It can only photosynthesize under certain conditions.
   b. It is only heterotrophic.
   c. It is both autotrophic and heterotrophic.
   d. It has no chloroplasts.

6. Members of the Kingdom Monera are found in our digestive tracts and perform which of the following functions?
   a. produce carbohydrates
   b. produce vitamins
   c. produce lipids
   d. produce proteins

► Answers

1. a. The abilities of fungi (and monerans) to engage in decomposition are critical for making nutrients available to new generations of plants.

2. d. Bacteria, largely because of their ability to rapidly reproduce asexually, are by far the most numerous organisms on Earth.

3. c. The bacteria in Kingdom Monera are responsible for converting atmospheric, gaseous nitrogen into chemical salts called nitrates that help fertilize plants.

4. a. Spores are produced as part of the reproductive cycle and are resistant to environmental conditions like temperature and moisture extremes.

5. c. Euglena can produce its own food through photosynthesis as plants do, and it can consume food as animals do. Euglena does contain chloroplasts that are the site of photosynthesis.

6. b. The bacteria in our digestive tracts are beneficial in the digestion of food, and they produce at least one vitamin, Vitamin K, which helps in the coagulation of blood.

► In Short

The general grouping of microorganisms (microbes) includes the bacteria (one-celled organisms without a true nucleus, also called prokaryotes) and the protists (one-celled organisms with a true nucleus, also called eukaryotes, along with all other organisms besides the bacteria). Single-celled fungi (yeasts) are also microorganisms, but multicelled fungi also exist in abundance. We are completely dependent upon the action of microorganisms, and many more of them are beneficial rather than harmful.

LESSON

5 ▶ Plants

You can usually tell plants from other organisms because they (or parts of their bodies) are green. This is because plants contain a molecule called *chlorophyll*. Chlorophyll acts as a pigment to give plants their green color, but more importantly, it absorbs sunlight energy in the first step of the process known as *photosynthesis*. Plants also have *chloroplasts* and *cell walls*. This lesson introduces the world of plants. Photosynthesis is introduced in a later lesson.

▶ What Is a Plant?

Many diverse organisms are classified within the Plant Kingdom, but they usually share certain characteristics that make them recognizable as plants. They are usually green (or part of their body is green), and they do not have the ability of locomotion, so they stay in one spot. They carry out the process known as *photosynthesis*, which turns carbon dioxide and water into sugars and oxygen gas. This process takes place in structures called *chloroplasts*. Plant cells have a hard cell wall made of the carbohydrate, *cellulose*.

Diverse Environments and Plants

Plants are found in nearly every place on Earth. They are located in the ocean and on mountaintops, they are in extremely warm and extremely cold places, and they even exist in very dry places like deserts. Plants are dependent upon light, so their access to a source of light is what limits where they can live. Water is also important to plant growth and development because much of plants' support comes from the water contained within its cells by the cell wall.

Long ago, two major groups of land plants evolved from algae, the *bryophytes* or nonvascular plants and the *tracheophytes* or vascular plants.

BRYOPHYTES (NONVASCULAR PLANTS)

These plants lack roots, leaves, and stems, but they do have structures called *rhizoids* (root-like hairs) that absorb water and nutrients. However, the bryophytes have no vessels for conducting water throughout their bodies, so they rely on slow diffusion to distribute water and nutrients. This means that they cannot grow very large because the process of diffusion would be too inefficient to support large bodies. The most representative plants in this grouping are the liverworts and mosses.

TRACHEOPHYTES

Trachea refers to *tube,* and these vascular plants have *tubes* (vessels) that provide support and a means of transporting water and nutrients throughout their bodies. Vascular plants can thus grow very tall, up to hundreds of feet. This group is further broken down into two types, the seedless vascular plants and the seeded vascular plants.

Seedless vascular plants include club mosses, horsetails, and ferns. These plants must be in moist environments because they need water to reproduce. Millions of years ago, these types of plants dominated the Earth, and they grew to large sizes. Many of these types of plants are still in existence, but the seed plants have become dominant. The remains of the many seedless plants from millions of years ago have been transformed into oil and coal by tremendous heat and pressure.

Seed plants have become dominant today because they have developed pollen and seeds as adaptations. *Pollen* is a protective structure that ensures that the sperm cell used in pollination survives harsh conditions until it reaches the female part of a flower and can fertilize the egg found there. *Seeds* are an adaptation that allows these plants to undergo a period of inactivity in their life cycles. The seed contains and protects an immature plant in a state of dormancy. The small plant stays dormant until conditions are favorable, and then it germinates and forms a new plant.

Seeds are also very highly adapted to many ways of being dispersed. Some seeds are distributed by wind, some by water, and others by animals. This dispersal is a way plants can establish themselves in new areas because they cannot transport themselves. Seed plants are divided into two groups, flowering and nonflowering plants.

Flowers and Cones

Gymnosperms is the name given to seed plants that do not form flowers. These plants were present on Earth before the flowering seed plants. Representatives of this group include pines, spruce, and cypresses. Gymnosperms are adapted to cold, dry areas. They have very thin, small leaves covered with a waterproof layer that keeps them from drying out. They also retain green leaves all year long (these are the plants we call *evergreens*) so that they can continue making food all year long. They also produce a kind of biological antifreeze in their sap that keeps them from freezing. This substance is what produces the scent from a pine tree, for example. Gymnosperms also produce seeds in cones.

Angiosperms is the name given to seed plants that do form flowers. These plants now dominate the Earth (even more so than the gymnosperms) and are highly diverse with many different types of plants. The angiosperms have been successful because they have developed flowers, fruits, and broad leaves. Their broad leaves allow them to capture more sunlight and produce more of their own food than the narrow, thin leaves of the gymnosperms.

Their most attractive characteristic is their flowers. *Flowers* are structures that contain the male and female sexual parts where sperm and egg cells are produced. The structure of flowers is designed to attract animals that will assist in the pollination process. Thus, flowers are colorful and fragrant. They also often offer a "reward" of nectar or pollen that the animal, such as a bee, uses for food.

Additionally, *fruits* are clearly important to animals and humans. They are also important to flowering seed plants because fruits are the remnants of the flower and contain the fully developed seed. The fleshy, sweet-tasting fruit encourages animals to eat them and disperse the seeds they contain.

▶ Practice

1. Which of the following characteristics is NOT a plant characteristic?
   a. They are able to engage in locomotion by moving from place to place.
   b. They use chlorophyll contained in chloroplasts.
   c. They produce sugars and oxygen.
   d. They use carbon dioxide and water in photosynthesis.

2. Which of the following plants are called bryophytes?
   a. horsetails
   b. ferns
   c. liverworts
   d. spruce trees

3. Which plant group now dominates the Earth?
   a. gymnosperms
   b. bryophytes
   c. seedless vascular plants
   d. angiosperms

4. Tracheophyte is another name for which type of plant?
   a. nonvascular plants
   b. only angiosperm plants
   c. only gymnosperm plants
   d. vascular plants

5. Which of the following strategies does an angiosperm plant NOT use to attract animals who act as pollinators?
   a. It produces pollen.
   b. It produces nectar.
   c. It produces chloroplasts.
   d. It produces fruit.

6. Plants in the bryophyte classification use rhizoids to act as what similar structure in vascular plants?
   a. leaves
   b. chloroplasts
   c. roots
   d. stems

▶ Answers

1. a. Plants are not able to move from one spot to another, although they can produce seeds that are easily dispersed from one spot to another. The other answers are characteristics that plants do exhibit and that separate plants from other organisms.

2. c. Liverworts and mosses are the most common representatives of the bryophytes that are plants that do not possess a vascular system. Horsetails and ferns are seedless vascular plants, and spruce trees are nonflowering seed plants.

3. d. Angiosperms, the flowering seed plants, are the dominant plant species. The other categories have many representatives and are quite successful in more limited habitats.

4. d. Racheophyte refers to plants with tubes or a vascular system. Nonvascular plants (the bryophytes: mosses and liverworts) are not tracheophytes. Angiosperms (flowering seed plants) and gymnosperms (nonflowering seed plants) are both tracheophytes.

5. c. Angiosperm (flowering) plants produce nectar, pollen, and fruit, which animals are attracted to as food sources. In the process of gathering or consuming these foods, the animal pollinators will be assisting in the plant's reproductive process. Chloroplasts are used in photosynthesis and not to attract animals.

6. c. Bryophytes are nonvascular plants that do not have actual roots but root-like structures called rhizoids.

▶ In Short

Many diverse organisms are classified within the Plant Kingdom, but they usually share certain characteristics that make them recognizable as plants. They are usually green (or part of their body is green), and they do not have the ability of locomotion, so they stay in one spot. They carry out the process known as photosynthesis, which turns carbon dioxide and water into sugars and oxygen gas. Long ago, two major groups of land plants evolved from algae, the bryophytes or nonvascular plants and the tracheophytes or vascular plants. Within vascular plants are two types, seedless and seeded. The seed plants also have two varieties, flowering and nonflowering.

6 ▶ Animals

Animals are multicelled, usually highly mobile, and unable to produce their own food like plants can. The Animal Kingdom is divided into two large groupings, the *invertebrates* (animals with no internal skeleton, although they may have an external skeleton called an *exoskeleton*), and *vertebrates* (animals with an internal skeleton and a highly evolved nervous system, such as humans).

▶ Animal Populations

Because birds and mammals are so large, obvious, and similar to us, we tend to think of them as being the dominant animals on Earth. The real picture is one in which smaller, less obvious, and boneless creatures are dominant. Such creatures are plentiful and have adapted to environments we cannot easily visit, such as the ocean depths. These animals are in the large group we call the *invertebrates*. We, along with other mammals, birds, fish, reptiles, and amphibians, are *vertebrates*. All the vertebrates together make up less than 5% of all the animal species on Earth; invertebrates make up the rest.

It is conjectured that colonies of protists whose members became specialized to perform certain roles eventually developed into the earliest form of animals. Today, the sponges, which live mostly in saltwater, are the closest example of organisms that are a collection of single-celled creatures. They have no specialized organs or tissues but maintain a well-defined shape and have a very rudimentary skeleton.

What Is an Animal?

From sponges to human beings, wherever they are found, animals share some fundamental characteristics. When an animal egg is fertilized, it undergoes several cell divisions or cleavages, quickly producing a cluster of cells called a *morula*. As cleavage continues, the morula develops into several distinct stages, reaching a stage called the *gastrula*, which is a double-layered simple embryo. From this gastrula, the full, multi-celled organism develops tissues and organ systems, and eventually develops into its adult form.

Immature as well as adult animals come in diverse forms. However, as multicellular animals, they all must come up with solutions to several basic problems, and these solutions give animals a different appearance from plants. The problems fall into several broad categories.

- **Surface-area-to-volume issues:** This issue is a matter of size. Nutrients, air, and water must be able to enter an animal's body to sustain life. This means that the surface area of an animal's body must be large enough to allow a sufficient amount of these elements to be used by the whole volume of the organism. In single-celled organisms, this means the cell size is strictly limited to the amount of nutrients that can pass through the cell membrane to support the whole volume of the cell. In multicelled organisms, specialized tissues and systems have evolved to bring in the necessary elements and then carry them to the cells. So it is not necessary for the body surface area of a large, multicelled animal to be able to supply all necessary elements. Specialized tissues and organ systems with very large surface areas have developed that absorb nutrients or air and filter wastes for the entire body. By working in conjunction with the circulatory system, these tissues and organs are able to support a large-sized (large-volume) multicelled body. The specialized tissues are found in the respiratory (breathing) system, urinary (excretory) system, and the digestive system.

- **Body support and protection:** All animals have some form of support and protection for their bodies. Sponges have a rudimentary skeletal network; crustaceans (such as crayfish) and insects have a hard outer coating called an *exoskeleton;* and mammals, birds, fish, reptiles, and amphibians have an internal skeleton. In all cases, these skeletal systems provide support to the animal's body and protect the internal organs from damage.

- **Locomotion:** Animals are heterotrophs and cannot produce their own food from exposure to sunlight, so they must acquire food. This need, as well as the need to mate and reproduce, forces an animal to move. Plants move but usually just in place, where they are rooted. Animals, on the other hand, move from place to place; this is called *locomotion.* Locomotion requires a muscular system, which animals came to develop in conjunction with the skeletal system to provide movement. Muscles are found as an adaptation only in animals, not in plants, fungi, or one-celled microorganisms.

- **Sensory integration**: Animals have complex bodies with many parts and systems that need coordination. This has resulted in the evolution of nervous tissue and, in many animals, a highly evolved nervous system, including a brain and spinal cord. In addition, animals have many specialized sensory organs (eyes, ears, noses, etc.) integrated into their nervous systems. These organs sense the environment and allow animals to show a very noticeable and marked response to environmental stimuli. The integration and coordination of sense organs, skeletal/muscular systems, and other bodily functions require an organized collection of specialized nervous tissue known as a *central nervous system*. The central nervous system has adapted into its most impressive form in human beings and other vertebrates.

Classifying Animals into Phyla

Phylum Porifera: sponges

Collections of individual cells, with no tissues or organs, and no nervous system or skeleton.

Phylum Coelenterata: jellyfish, sea anemones, coral

Usually very beautiful forms, their bodies are two-layered and symmetrical in a circular fashion with rudimentary organs and systems, but no skeleton.

Phylum Platyhelminthes: flatworms, tapeworms

Their bodies are symmetrical in a left/right fashion (like humans). Their bodies have three layers and have very rudimentary nervous tissue.

Phylum Nematoda: roundworms

They are symmetrical like the flatworms and have three body layers. Many are beneficial soil organisms, whereas some are parasites (such as hookworms and pinworms).

Phylum Annelida: segmented worms

These have bodies similar to other previous worms but with some more advanced characteristics, including sensory organs and a relatively developed nervous system. Their bodies are divided into segments; earthworms are the best example of animals in this category.

Phylum Echinodermata: sea stars and sea urchins

Their bodies have a circular symmetry with five body parts being arranged around a central axis. They have calcium spines or plates just under the skin and a unique water vascular system that is a series of fluid-filled vessels that provide body support and allow for locomotion.

Phylum Mollusca: snails, clams, and octopuses

These have a well-developed circulatory system, nervous system, and digestive system; octopuses have particularly well-developed brains with highly maneuverable tentacles.

Phylum Arthropoda: crustaceans, spiders, and insects

This phylum has more species than the other phylums, mostly because of all the insect species. Their bodies have exoskeletons, and most undergo metamorphosis (a transformation that allows them to grow by shedding their exoskeleton and developing into a larger or more adult form). They often have specialized body parts (antennae, pinchers, etc.), and they are well adapted to many environments.

Phylum Chordata: amphibians, reptiles, fish, birds, and mammals (including humans)

These are the most familiar animals, and we all share four characteristics: a notochord that often develops into the vertebral column in vertebrates; a nerve cord that runs along our backs; gill slits at some point in our development; and a tail or at least a vestigial tail (humans have the tailbone or coccyx).

► Practice

1. Multicellular animals have developed respiratory and excretory (urinary) systems because they need to overcome which of the following issues?
   a. weight versus mass
   b. surface area to volume
   c. height to weight
   d. mass to volume

2. Animals are divided into which of the following two categories?
   a. single celled and multicelled
   b. autotrophic and heterotrophic
   c. mobile and immobile
   d. vertebrate and invertebrate

3. Jellyfish and coral are related to what other animal?
   a. octopus
   b. sea anemone
   c. sea urchin
   d. sponges

4. The Phylum Arthropoda contains which of the following animals?
   a. spiders
   b. sea stars
   c. sponges
   d. seals

5. Phylum Annelida contains which of the following animals?
   a. flatworms
   b. sponges
   c. round worms
   d. segmented worms

6. Humans are classified under which of the following Phyla?
   a. Echinodermata
   b. Chordata
   c. Mollusca
   d. Platyhelminthes

▶ Answers

1. b. Single-celled organisms can exchange gases and fluids directly across their cell membranes because their volume is not too large for the surface area of their cell membranes to have a good exchange rate. Because multicellular animals have a large volume compared to single-celled animals, they must come up with ways to increase the surface area of exchange membranes. In the respiratory system, they have a huge surface area in their lungs for the exchange of gases, and in the urinary system, the kidneys also have a huge surface area for the exchange of fluids.

2. d. The multicellular bodies of animals can either have a backbone contained in a vertebral column (the vertebrates) or not (the invertebrates). The invertebrates far outnumber the vertebrates, even though the latter may be more obvious and familiar.

3. b. The octopus is a mollusk, the sea urchin is an echinoderm, and the sponge is in the Phylum Porifera. The sea anemone is a coelenterate like the jellyfish and coral.

4. a. Spiders are classified under Arthropoda, sea stars are under Echinodermata, sponges are under Porifera, and seals are under Chordata.

5. d. Segmented worms (like earthworms) are classified under Annelida, flatworms are under Platyhelminthes, sponges are under Porifera, and roundworms are under Nematoda.

6. b. Humans are chordates.

▶ In Short

As multicellular animals, animals must come up with solutions to several basic problems. These solutions give animals a different appearance from plants. These problems fall into several broad categories: surface-area-to-volume issues, body support and protection, locomotion, and sensory integration. Animals are also organized into several phyla.

LESSON

7 ▶ Ecosystems

The study of living organisms and the ways in which they interact with their physical environment and each other is called *ecology*. All these relationships form an *ecosystem*. The physical environment includes the type of soils, the amount of sunshine and rainfall, the weather and climate, the topography (or shape) of the land, and many other factors. An organism's habitat provides for the needs of that organism. Large areas of the earth and its oceans share similar habitats and physical environment characteristics. These areas are called *biomes*, and because they include the relationships of many organisms and physical factors, they are also ecosystems.

▶ Biosphere and Biome

Earth is a large planet, and much of its bulk is not suitable for living organisms, but three factors interact to make life possible. These three factors are air, water, and rock (or soil). We also refer to these factors as being the atmosphere (air), hydrosphere (water), and lithosphere (rocks and soil). An interaction takes place between these physical factors and the life of Earth to create an environment we call the *biosphere*. The biosphere contains all of Earth's living organisms. Large areas of the earth (both on land and in water) may contain several small living systems operating in a region with definable conditions. These large areas are called *biomes*. Each biome has organisms and physical environment characteristics that define it. Several biomes have been identified and defined.

▶ Ecosystem

We define an ecosystem as being all the relationships between organisms in a defined area and their interactions with their physical environment. An ecosystem can be very large, including the entire Earth (in which case, we refer to it as the biosphere) or the large regions we call biomes. However, ecosystems can also be very small; even a single tree can be the foundation of a whole ecosystem, and a terrarium or aquarium is a model of an ecosystem you can create yourself. No matter the size or form of an ecosystem, groups of organisms will affect and be affected by each other and their physical surroundings.

The living organisms in an ecosystem are collectively known as the *biotic* (biological) component, whereas the nonliving things such as water, minerals, and sunlight are collectively known as the *abiotic* (nonbiological) component. Studying the interactions between the biotic and abiotic components helps us understand an ecosystem.

The particular details of one ecosystem will differ when compared to another. They will have different organisms present or different abiotic factors available. But in all cases, ecosystems exhibit two primary features:

1. a single direction to the flow of energy, in the form of chemical bonds, from photosynthetic organisms, like green plants or algae, to animals that eat the plants or other animals.
2. the cycling of inorganic minerals, such as nitrogen, calcium, and phosphorous, through living organisms and then back to the environment. The return of these inorganic materials to the environment happens largely by the action of organisms known as *decomposers* (such as bacteria and fungi). Other organisms called *detritivores* (such as pillbugs, sowbugs, millipedes, and earthworms) help break down large pieces of organic matter into smaller pieces that the decomposers then work on.

A complete definition of an ecosystem could be stated as a combination of biotic and abiotic components through which energy flows and inorganic material recycles.

▶ Requirements of Organisms

Every organism needs food, water, and shelter, which must come from the area in which it lives. This area is called an organism's *habitat*. Within its habitat, an organism has a function or role to play to help maintain the community. The role of some organisms is to capture sunlight and produce food compounds. We call these organisms plants or *autotrophs*, a word that roughly translates as one who feeds oneself. We also call plants *producers* because they produce their own food. Other organisms eat plants and some eat each other. These organisms are called *heterotrophs*, which means eater of others. We also call heterotrophs consumers, and most animals are in this group because they must consume food (they cannot make their own). Still other organisms, such as pillbugs, eat the leftover remains or droppings of other organisms. These organisms are referred to as *detritivores*, which means eater of detritus (leaf litter).

An Organism's Niche

The roles an organism plays in a community and how it affects and is affected by its habitat are the factors that determine an organism's niche. An easy way to understand the concept of a niche is to think of it as being an organism's "location" and "occupation" within a community. For example, birds and squirrels both live in a tree habitat, but they do not occupy the same niche because they eat different foods. Their "locations" are the same, but they have different food-gathering abilities and requirements as their "occupations."

▶ **Practice**

1. Ecology is the study of organisms interacting with
   a. the physical environment only.
   b. the internal environment only.
   c. the physical environment and each other.
   d. each other and the internal environment.

2. In terms of energy, an ecosystem is defined as
   a. moving energy back and forth between organisms.
   b. moving energy in one direction from plants to animals.
   c. not utilizing energy.
   d. moving energy in one direction from animals to plants.

3. Decomposers are important because they
   a. recycle nutrients.
   b. produce sugars.
   c. produce oxygen.
   d. engage in asexual reproduction.

4. Which of the following best describes the concept of an organism's niche?
   a. It is the organism's function or "occupation" in an ecosystem.
   b. It is the organism's location or "address" in an ecosystem.
   c. It is both an organism's function and location in an ecosystem.
   d. It is the binomial classification of an organism in an ecosystem.

5. Pillbugs consume dead organic matter and are most accurately described by the name
   a. decomposers.
   b. detritivores.
   c. producers.
   d. autotroph.

▶ Answers

1. c. Ecology studies the ways in which organisms interact with each other and their physical environment.

2. b. Energy within an ecosystem is captured by green plants through photosynthesis and is then passed on to animals when they eat the plants or each other.

3. a. The cycling of inorganic minerals, such as nitrogen, calcium, and phosphorous, through living organisms and then back to the environment happens largely by the action of organisms known as decomposers (such as bacteria and fungi). Other organisms called detritivores (such as pillbugs, sowbugs, millipedes, and earthworms) help break down large pieces of organic matter into smaller pieces that the decomposers then work on.

4. c. The concept of a niche includes both what the organism does in an ecosystem (its function or "occupation") as well as its actual physical location ("address") within the ecosystem.

5. b. Pillbugs are called detritivores because they eat dead organic matter such as leaves, which are also called detritus (litter on the forest floor).

▶ In Short

The study of living organisms and the ways in which they interact with their physical environment and each other is called ecology. All these relationships form an ecosystem. In all cases, ecosystems exhibit two primary features:

1. a single direction to the flow of energy, in the form of chemical bonds, from photosynthetic organisms, such as green plants or algae, to animals that eat the plants or other animals.

2. the cycling of inorganic minerals, such as nitrogen, calcium, and phosphorous, through living organisms and then back to the environment. The return of these inorganic materials to the environment happens largely by the action of organisms known as decomposers (such as bacteria and fungi) and others called detritivores (such as pillbugs, sowbugs, millipedes, and earthworms).

A complete definition of an ecosystem could be stated as a combination of biotic and abiotic components through which energy flows and inorganic material recycles.

8 ▶ Ecology: Organisms and Their Interactions

When we talk about the relationships among organisms in an ecosystem, the most important is how they relate to each other as predators and prey. The best means of illustrating these relationships is through food chains and food webs.

▶ Food Chains

Food chains don't just show who eats whom, but instead, they represent the flow of energy contained in the chemical bonds of food molecules. When a fox eats a rabbit, the chemical bonds that make up the tissues of the rabbit's body will be broken down by the digestive system of the fox. This digestive process releases energy and smaller chemical molecules that the fox's body uses to make more fox tissue. Likewise, before the fox eats the rabbit, it uses the food energy in grass and plants to gain energy for its own life processes.

Let's look at a simple food chain such as one that includes grass, grasshoppers, frogs, and raccoons. Sunlight energy enters the food chain during a series of chemical reactions called *photosynthesis*. These reactions take place in plant tissue. The plant uses this sunlight energy to make food molecules, which are stored within the tissues of the plant. When the grasshopper eats the plant, it consumes some of the food molecules and uses these molecules in its own body. An organism at the next level of the food chain, such as the frog, then eats the grasshopper and derives energy from the tissue of the grasshopper. A series of these steps from one organism to the next is called a food chain.

Food Webs

A *food web* is a more complex view of energy transmission that includes more predator-prey relationships between more organisms. Food chains are parts of food webs. Each step along a food chain or within a food web represents what is called a *trophic* (or feeding) *level*. The first step in any food chain or the first trophic level is always a photosynthetic organism. These organisms, such as plants in terrestrial ecosystems and algae in aquatic ecosystems, use light from the sun, water, carbon dioxide, and a few minerals to produce food molecules. The chemical bonds in food molecules represent captured energy that can then be available to fuel the whole food chain. Organisms at this first trophic level are known as *primary producers*. See the following illustration of a food web.

Energy and Food Webs

Energy becomes a part of the animal communities through those who eat plants. These organisms are called *herbivores* and, because they are at the second trophic level, are also known as *primary consumers*. Herbivores (primary consumers) eat plants and derive energy for their own life processes. However, much of the energy that transfers from the first trophic level to the second level (or from primary producers to primary consumers) is not turned into herbivore tissue but is instead lost as heat, used in the digestive process itself or used for movement by the herbivore. Much of the plant material is not even digested, so it passes through the digestive system and is excreted as waste. This waste material still contains much energy in the chemical bonds that make up the material.

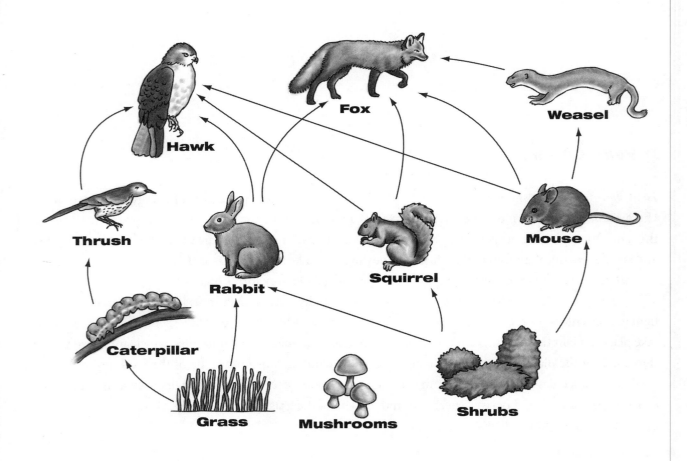

Because much of the energy available from the primary producers (plants) does not become part of an herbivore's body mass, a given amount of plant material would not be able to sustain as many herbivores as you might think. As you move from one trophic level to another, it is usually estimated that only 10% of the available energy gets turned into body tissue at the next higher level. As a simple example, consider a field that has 100 pounds of plants. In terms of the energy available, you might think this field could provide for 100 pounds of rabbits, but the reality is that it would only be able to support a group of rabbits that weighs a total of ten pounds. The loss of 90% of the energy to other factors results in only one or two rabbits. If you then move to the next higher trophic level, a rabbit will only provide enough energy to sustain one pound of a fox's body. Again, the loss of 90% of the energy yields not even enough left over to completely sustain a fox, but only to sustain the fox for a short period of time.

▶ Practice

1. The steps in a food chain or food web are called _____ and represent the _____ of an organism.
   a. biome levels; energy level
   b. trophic levels; energy level
   c. trophic levels; feeding level
   d. energy levels; feeding level

2. In this food chain,

grass → rabbit → fox

how much of the energy captured in the grass's tissue is available to the fox?
   a. 100%
   b. 50%
   c. 10%
   d. 1%

3. Another term for herbivores is
   a. plants.
   b. second-order consumers.
   c. first-order consumers
   d. third trophic-level organisms.

4. Several interacting food chains form a
   a. food pyramid.
   b. food web.
   c. food column.
   d. food triangle.

5. Herbivores are at the second trophic level and can also be called
   a. primary producers.
   b. primary consumers.
   c. secondary consumers.
   d. secondary producers.

▶ Answers

1. c. Each step is a trophic level, which represents the feeding position or level where an organism exists in a particular food chain or food web. The word trophic refers to feeding (or eating).

2. d. In each step of a food chain, only 10% of the energy moves from one trophic level to the next. If the grass represents 100% of the energy available, then the rabbit would only have 10% available, and the fox would then only have 1% available. In other words, it would take 100 pounds of grass to support ten pounds of rabbit and then one pound of fox.

3. c. An herbivore is an animal that eats plants. Plants are producers in food chains, and any organism that eats plants is a consumer. Animals that eat other animals are also consumers. All animals are some kind of consumer because they cannot make their own food. First-order consumers such as herbivores are at the second level of a food chain (plants are at the first level), but they are the first level of consumer. Second-order consumers are other animals that eat herbivores. Third trophic-level organisms are another way of saying second-order consumers (they are at the third trophic level after herbivores and plants).

4. b. Food webs are complex groupings of interacting food chains. Organisms may play different roles in different food chains. Food webs with a number of diverse organisms are considered more stable than single food chains.

5. b. Primary consumers are the first level of consumers, but also the second trophic level. The first trophic level contains the producers (plants).

▶ In Short

Organisms interact with each other, and the most common interaction is within the structure of a food chain in which one organism is the food and energy source for another organism. All food chains start with plants as producers because they can photosynthesize and capture sunlight energy. Animals are consumers and eat either plants or each other. Several food chains can be interwoven to create a food web in which many organisms interact with each other.

Biochemistry: Photosynthesis and Respiration

The process of photosynthesis performed by plants is the fundamental way Earth's life interacts with the nonliving, physical environment. Photosynthesis takes lifeless energy along with inorganic, inanimate chemicals and converts them into organic matter that feeds all life forms. In a companion set of reactions, animals (and plants) use organic matter and oxygen to derive energy to live. This is called *respiration*.

▶ A Plant Experiment

Around the mid-1600s, a Dutch doctor, Johann Baptista van Helmont (1579–1644), planted a willow tree. He did his planting as part of a controlled experiment, so he carefully weighed the plant, the soil, and the amount of water he used. After several years, the plant had gained over 150 pounds, but the weight of the soil had not changed. To van Helmont and people of his day, this result showed that the water had been turned into the matter of the tree. It wasn't until the end of the following century, more than a hundred years later, that we discovered the real weight gain came from the plant absorbing gasses from the air and using those with energy from sunlight to grow in size.

Photosynthesis

The biochemical process that plants use to grow and gain weight is called *photosynthesis,* which is a highly necessary instance of a biochemical reaction. In this process, plants absorb carbon dioxide from the air and form a union of this gas with water, using sunlight energy and specialized chemicals called *enzymes.* The process allows the plants to produce sugar (glucose) and oxygen.

Photosynthesis Equation

Written using the chemist's shorthand, the photosynthesis equation looks like this:

$$6CO_2 + 6H_2O \xrightarrow{\text{enzymes and sunlight}} C_6H_{12}O_6 + 6O_2$$

Metabolism

Metabolism is the collection of all the physical and chemical processes in which a living being is engaged. Metabolism is one of the functions that distinguishes life from nonlife. Living beings maintain themselves at a complex level of organization, and metabolism helps them do this. Nonliving objects are more simply constructed and do not engage in metabolism.

Turning Energy into Matter

The really fascinating aspect of photosynthesis is that raw sunlight energy, a very nonliving thing, is absorbed by plants to form the chemical bonds between simple, inanimate compounds that yield an organic foodstuff (the sugar) upon which all life is dependent. This sugar, called *glucose*, is the chemical basis for the formation all living compounds. Plants use other biochemical reactions to turn glucose into useful molecules, and herbivore animals that eat plants use glucose and other plant-based compounds to create the molecules they need. Carnivorous animals that eat other animals also form compounds from those food molecules, but at the basis of it all is the capture and conversion of sunlight energy into organic matter during photosynthesis.

What about That Oxygen?

The other endproduct of photosynthesis besides glucose is the gas oxygen. Most organisms, especially the ones we are most familiar with, require oxygen to help fuel the biochemical reactions of metabolism, and even plants themselves use oxygen in their metabolism. Respiration is a reaction that uses oxygen, but more accurately, we refer to it as *aerobic respiration*, because aerobic refers to air (or oxygen). Respiration is the metabolic opposite of photosynthesis.

Respiration

Respiration is defined as the reaction that uses enzymes to combine oxygen with organic matter (food) in order to yield carbon dioxide, water, and energy. Glucose is not the only foodstuff used in respiration, but it represents a good example.

Respiration Equation

In chemical shorthand, respiration looks like this:

$$C_6H_{12}O_6 + 6O_2 \xrightarrow{\text{enzymes}} 6CO_2 + 6H_2O + \text{energy}$$

If you look back at the equation for photosynthesis, you will see that the respiration equation is its opposite.

Respiration

It can be confusing to use the word respiration because that often also refers to the process of breathing. To avoid confusion, it might be better to think of breathing as inspiration and exhalation. Respiration, in that case, is the metabolic, chemical reaction. Additionally, both plants and animals produce carbon dioxide through respiration.

Another form of respiration is called *anaerobic,* where oxygen is not used. Aerobic respiration allows for a more complete breakdown of the chemical bonds in the food, thus releasing more energy. Therefore, it is the preferred way for multicelled animals to obtain energy for their large and complex bodies, whereas simpler, usually one-celled organisms use the far less energy-producing process of anaerobic respiration. This forms a neat metabolic cycle in which plants convert energy into matter and release oxygen gas. Animals then absorb this gas to run their metabolic reaction and, in the process, release carbon dioxide that the plants use in the photosynthetic conversion of energy into matter.

Chlorophyll and Light

Plants have a special molecule called *chlorophyll* that is used to capture the sunlight energy needed for photosynthesis. Chlorophyll absorbs sunlight, and one of its electrons is stimulated into a higher energy state. This electron passes energy on to other electrons in other molecules in a chain that eventually results in glucose. Oxygen is also released along the way. Chlorophyll absorbs red and blue light very strongly, but it does not absorb green light very well, so the green portion of sunlight is reflected back and our eyes see it. Thus, this is the reason plants look green.

▶ A Word about Enzymes

Chemical reactions generally happen more quickly when heat is applied. In living organisms, lots of heat would be harmful or fatal, so instead, they use enzymes. These molecules speed up reactions by bringing reactants closer together, causing them to form a new compound. Thus, the whole reaction is speeded without heat. Enzymes are not consumed in the reaction and can be used over and over as an important part of the biochemistry of photosynthesis and respiration.

▶ Practice

1. We now know that van Helmont reached the wrong conclusion in his experiment. Which of the following statements more accurately describes what occurred?
   a. The tree gained mass only by absorbing lots of water.
   b. The tree gained mass by absorbing carbon dioxide and water.
   c. The tree gained mass by absorbing some of the soil.
   d. The tree gained mass only by absorbing sunlight.

2. Which of the following is NOT true of enzymes?
   a. Enzymes are lipid molecules.
   b. Enzymes are not consumed in a biochemical reaction.
   c. Enzymes are important in photosynthesis and respiration.
   d. Enzymes speed up reactions and make them more efficient.

3. Plants look green to our eyes because chlorophyll
   a. absorbs green light.
   b. reflects red light.
   c. absorbs blue light.
   d. reflects green light.

4. Photosynthesis is the metabolic opposite of which of these processes?
   a. enzymatic hydrolysis
   b. protein synthesis
   c. respiration
   d. reproduction

5. The compound that absorbs light energy during photosynthesis is
   a. chloroform.
   b. chlorofluorocarbon.
   c. chlorinated biphenyls.
   d. chlorophyll.

6. Which of the following is the name of the sugar molecule made during photosynthesis?
   a. chlorophyll
   b. glycogen
   c. glucose
   d. fructose

▶ Answers

1. **b.** The tree absorbed water, which added to its mass, but the tissues of the tree needed the carbon from carbon dioxide to grow and develop. The other answers are incomplete or simply wrong.
2. **a.** Enzymes are protein molecules; the other statements are true of enzymes.
3. **d.** Because chlorophyll strongly absorbs red and blue light, the light in the green portion of the spectrum is reflected back to our eyes, and the plant thus appears green.
4. **c.** Respiration and photosynthesis are opposite metabolic reactions.
5. **d.** chlorophyll
6. **c.** glucose

▶ In Short

The biochemical process plants use to grow and gain weight is called photosynthesis. This is a highly necessary instance of a biochemical reaction. During photosynthesis, a plant takes in carbon dioxide and water while using sunlight and enzymes to produce glucose (a food molecule) and oxygen. Written using the chemist's shorthand, the photosynthesis equation looks like this:

enzymes and sunlight

$$6CO_2 + 6H_2O \longrightarrow C_6H_{12}O_6 + 6O_2$$

In a companion set of reactions, animals (and plants) use organic matter and oxygen to derive energy to live. This is called respiration, which combines oxygen with organic matter (food) using enzymes to yield carbon dioxide, water, and energy. Glucose is not the only foodstuff used in respiration, but it represents a good example. In chemical shorthand, respiration looks like this:

enzymes

$$C_6H_{12}O_6 + 6O_2 \longrightarrow 6CO_2 + 6H_2O + energy$$

10 ▶ Cells, Tissues, and Organs

One of the hallmark characteristics of living things is that they perform chemical reactions. These reactions are collectively known as *metabolism*. *Cells,* the basic units of life, can perform many of these metabolic reactions. In a multicelled organism, the cells group together to form *tissues* that perform the same functions. Tissues group together to form *organs,* and finally, several organs exist together in a system. In this lesson, we will see how and why this hierarchy is established.

▶ The Basic Unit of Life

All organisms from the smallest single-celled protists to huge whales and giant redwood trees are based on tiny microscopic cells. The types and number of cells may vary, but the *cell* is the basic unit of life.

The cell is the minimum amount of organized living matter complex enough to carry out the functions of life as outlined in Lessons 1 and 2. In the most basic sense, a cell is made of a gelatinous living substance we call *protoplasm*, which contains many small structures, all surrounded by a membrane.

Cell Structure

The *cell membrane* separates the living cell from the rest of the environment. However, this membrane is not just a static solid wall. It must allow food molecules and oxygen to enter and wastes to exit. Thus, the cell membrane is *semipermeable* because it allows some things to pass through, but not others. It must also communicate and associate with the membranes of other cells.

Inside the cell membrane is a substance called *protoplasm* in which many tiny structures called *organelles* (because they act like small versions of organs) are suspended. Some of the more important organelles and their functions are listed in the following table.

Cellular Differentiation

Simple, one-celled organisms use a single cell to carry out all the necessary biochemical and structural functions. However, in multicelled animals, except very primitive ones (such as sponges), different types of cells are specialized to perform a particular function. Thus, a division of labor takes place; some cells do one task while others do another. This kind of specialization leads to groups of cells equally specialized for a specific function. These grouped cells are known as *tissues*.

ORGANELLE	FUNCTION
Mitochondria	spherical or rod-shaped organelles that are nicknamed the "powerhouse" of the cell because they are responsible for carrying out the reactions of aerobic respiration, which yields energy
Ribosomes	extremely tiny spheres that are the site for protein production
Golgi apparatus	a layered stack of flattened sacs that is important in the production of polysaccharides (carbohydrates)
Endoplasmic reticulum	a complex system of internal membranes that is called rough when the ribosomes are attached, and smooth when they aren't
Chloroplasts	these contain the chlorophyll molecule used in photosynthesis and are only found in plants, not animals; they are the organelle of photosynthesis
Nucleus	a centrally located organelle that contains the genetic information as coded in the molecule DNA. It controls all the cell's functions

▶ Tissue Types

Tissues in plants and animals are categorized by their functions as shown in the following tables.

PLANT TISSUE TYPE	FUNCTION
Meristematic tissue	This consists of undifferentiated cells that have the ability to grow and divide; this tissue is located in the plant's growth regions (branch tips, roots, etc.).
Parenchyma, cholenchyma, and sclerenchyma tissues	These are used for support and nourishment, making up the main bulk of the plant's body; they give it strength and allow for the storage of food molecules.
Protective tissue	This helps the plant ward off disease, pests, and injury. It also protects the plant from drying out; an example is the waxy cuticle layer on leaves.
Conductive tissue	This is used to conduct or transport liquids and dissolved or suspended solids through the plant's body. This tissue goes from the roots through the stems and leaves. Sap is transported through the tube structures of this tissue. The main types of this tissue are xylem and phloem.

ANIMAL TISSUE TYPE	FUNCTION
Epithelial tissue	This is made up of flattened cells tightly grouped together to form a solid surface; skin is a good example. This tissue covers the body and protects it from injury. It also allows for the exchange of gases in the lungs and bronchial tubes, as well as the exchange of materials in the intestines. A form of epithelial tissue produces the sex cells (eggs and sperm).
Connective tissue	This is made up of cells surrounded by a lot of extracellular material not made of cells; cartilage and bones are good examples. Bone and cartilage have some cells, but they are surrounded by lots of noncellular material.
Nervous tissue	This is made of cells called *neurons* specialized to transmit electrical impulses; these cells make many connections with each other. The brain, spinal cord, and peripheral nerves are made of nervous tissue.
Contractile tissue	This has the ability to contract and occurs in three types: *cardiac* tissue found in the heart, *smooth* tissue found in the intestinal tract, and *skeletal* (or striated) tissue found in the muscles.

▶ Organs and Organ Systems

As living organisms go through their life cycle from birth to death, they gain mass or grow, and their bodies change or develop. Single-celled organisms grow and develop very rapidly, whereas more complex, multicelled organisms take much longer. Organisms go through some very large changes as they age. Humans start out as a single fertilized cell and then grow and develop over several years to the adult stage. This growth and development is a process that separates life from nonlife. It also makes it necessary to group tissues together into larger units called *organs*. The organs perform more complicated functions than do the single tissues that make them up.

For example, the heart is made of cardiac muscle (a type of contractile tissue) with its valves made of conjunctive tissue. This allows the heart to have a specific shape and to beat in a complicated way that delivers blood to the lungs for oxygenation and then throughout the body. Simple cardiac tissue not grouped into a heart organ would not be able to do this.

As another example, look at tree roots as organs. They have a protective epidermis (a "skin") made of protective tissue that covers them. They also are composed of meristematic tissue that allows them to grow. Also part of the root organ is conductive tissue because roots are meant to absorb and transport water and nutrients to the rest of the plant. Other examples of organs found in plants are flowers and leaves. In animals, however, many organs can be found, such as the brain, lungs, stomach, liver, eyes, ears, and so on.

Generally, in complex organisms like plants and animals, many organs are then grouped together into *systems*. A good example of an organ system is the digestive system in animals that consists of many organs (which in turn consist of many combinations of tissues). The digestive system contains the mouth, esophagus, stomach, small and large intestines, liver, pancreas, and gall bladder, to name some of the most well-known organs.

▶ Practice

1. Which of the following are true about organisms on Earth?

   a. All organisms are based on the cell as the basic unit of life.

   b. Protists are an exception to the cell theory and are not based on cells.

   c. Only single-celled organisms are based on cells.

   d. All organisms are based on tissues as the basic unit of life.

2. The organelle nicknamed the "powerhouse" of the cell is the

   a. chloroplast.

   b. nucleus.

   c. mitochondrion.

   d. endoplasmic reticulum.

3. The formation of tissue depends upon

   a. cell differentiation.

   b. cell membranes.

   c. cell death.

   d. cell organelles.

4. Cardiac muscle is an example of what kind of tissue?

   a. smooth muscle

   b. nervous

   c. contractile

   d. connective

5. Which organelle is a complex system of internal membranes that is called rough when ribosomes are attached and smooth when they aren't?

   a. mitochondrion

   b. Golgi apparatus

   c. nucleus

   d. endoplasmic reticulum

6. Which organelle is a layered stack of flattened sacs important in the production of polysaccharides (carbohydrates)?

   a. mitochondrion

   b. Golgi apparatus

   c. nucleus

   d. endoplasmic reticulum

▶ Answers

1. a. All organisms are based on the cell as the basic unit of life; the other statements are incomplete or incorrect.

2. c. The mitochondrion is called the cell's "power-house" because it is the site of aerobic respiration and the release of energy from the chemical bonds of food molecules.

3. a. The differentiation of cells into specialized functional groupings leads to tissues.

4. c. A cardiac muscle is an example of contractile tissue.

5. d. endoplasmic reticulum

6. b. Golgi apparatus

▶ In Short

Cells are the basic unit of life. All living organisms are made of cells. Some cells, like those of bacteria, are very simple, yet they perform a wide range of functions. Other cells are more elaborately constructed, but may perform only one function because they are part of a larger organism, where many cells combine to perform the necessary functions of life. All cells are microscopic in size, and there are many types of cells. In larger, multi-ticelled organisms, cells can specialize in their functions, which creates a division of labor. Some cells perform one thing while others do another. This kind of specialization leads to groups of cells equally specialized in a function. These grouped cells are known as tissues.

We each start out as a single fertilized cell, and we then grow and develop over several years to our adult stage. This growth and development is a process that separates life from nonlife. It also makes it necessary to group tissues together into larger units called organs, which perform more complicated functions than do the single tissues that make them up. Generally, in complex organisms like plants and animals, many organs are then grouped together into specific systems.

LESSON 11

Nutrition and Energy Use: The Digestive System

All organisms need nutritious food to live. Our digestive system takes in foodstuffs by first grinding them into small pieces by chewing and stomach action. Then the small bits participate in chemical reactions that yield the specific substances our bodies need. The chemical reactions of digestion are dependent upon molecules we call *enzymes*. Once the digestive process yields the specific substances our bodies need, they must be absorbed, and our digestive tract has been developed to do that. Absorption also depends on lots of surface area.

► Cellular Metabolism

To sustain themselves, living organisms must consume organic matter (or food). The biochemical reactions of metabolism use food as energy and these reactions occur at the cellular level. The two main types of reactions are *anabolism* and *catabolism*.

You may have heard of the anabolic steroids that athletes take to improve their performance. These substances work because they stimulate the process of anabolism in which simple molecules are built into more complex ones. For athletes, it helps build more muscle tissue. Anabolism is thus a constructive process, and anabolic processes require energy. Conversely, catabolism is a destructive process in which complex molecules are broken down into simpler ones, releasing energy as chemical bonds are broken.

Both processes require a substance that speeds up the reaction. Such a substance is called an *enzyme*, which can also be described as a *biological catalyst*. Energy for living beings is contained in the chemical bonds of food molecules. To begin with, plant photosynthesis captures sunlight energy and locks it into the chemical bonds of organic matter. Once an animal consumes this matter, it is usually broken down (by catabolism) into simple molecules, and energy is released from the chemical bonds in the organic matter. An organism then uses those simple molecules and some of the energy to rebuild complex molecules (by anabolism) into the ones it needs.

Digestive System

Before the cells can use food for energy, the large molecules we eat must be broken down into smaller ones that can be absorbed by the body and distributed to the cells in a usable form. It is the digestive system's job to break down foodstuffs using chemical and mechanical processes. The circulatory system then aids in the distribution of small organic molecules to the body's cells. The digestive system is essentially a long, hollow tube around which the rest of the body is built. This tube in vertebrates is open at one end (the mouth) for the ingestion of food and open at the other end (the anus) for the elimination of wastes. Along the length of the tube are accessory organs that have important functions in digestion. All of these chemical reactions, whether catabolic or anabolic, are catalyzed by enzymes.

The first step in the process of digestion is for the food to be broken down into a fine mash or pulp. In this form, the food has a much greater surface area, and the fine particles are more exposed to digestive enzymes and other fluids. This starts in the mouth where chewing breaks food down and saliva moistens it to form a pulpy mass. Enzymes in the saliva immediately begin working to break down starches and complex carbohydrates into simple sugars.

After chewing, food is swallowed as a lump called a *bolus,* which passes through the *esophagus* (a tube that connects the mouth to the stomach). The smooth muscle that lines the esophagus contracts and relaxes in such a way to move the food along. We call these rhythmic contractions *peristalsis.*

In the stomach, food breakdown continues. Gastric pits in the wall of the stomach secrete strong acid and enzymes. These chemicals are especially good at breaking down proteins into smaller chains of amino acids. The walls of the stomach begin contracting to mix the food and digestive fluids. After a couple hours, the food mass has been turned into a pasty mixture called *chyme.* At this point, the chyme is ready to pass from the stomach into the small intestine. However, only some starches have been broken down into simpler sugars, and the proteins have been broken down into smaller chains of amino acids.

In the small intestine, a variety of enzymes are added to the chyme mixture, and the still undigested food is broken down into absorbable molecules. Many accessory organs such as the liver, pancreas, and gall bladder contribute enzymes and buffering fluids to the mix inside the small intestine to aid in the chemical breakdown of food. The small intestine is quite long, up to 21 or more feet in adult humans and even larger in other animals. Also, peristaltic muscular action is still responsible for moving the food along.

In addition to its length, the interior wall of the small intestine is folded in such a way as to greatly increase the surface area. Small projections or foldings of the inner wall called *villi* (*villus* is the singular form) look like little fingers extending into the interior of the small intestine. The surface of each villus is further folded into *microvilli.* All this surface area makes the absorption of food molecules very efficient. Each villus has its own tiny blood vessels, and food molecules move through the villi cells into the blood stream for distribution to the rest of the body.

At the end of the small intestine, most nutrients that the vertebrate body needs have been absorbed. What remains is mostly water, cellulose (from the plant tissue eaten), and other indigestible matter. This mass passes into the large intestine or colon. The main function of the colon is to absorb water, reducing the undigested matter into solid waste called *feces*, which is eliminated from the body in a bowel movement.

▶ Practice

1. The function of the digestive system is to break down food molecules and distribute them to the body so that
   a. the liver can break down starches.
   b. the cells can break down proteins.
   c. the lungs can engage in respiration.
   d. the cells can engage in cellular respiration.

2. Chyme enters the small intestine
   a. devoid of all nutritional value.
   b. with all food molecules completely broken down.
   c. with some food molecules partially broken down.
   d. where it is not exposed to enzymes.

3. Once food reaches the cells, it is subjected to cellular respiration and what other two metabolic processes?
   a. circulation and breathing
   b. anabolism and catabolism
   c. integration and summation
   d. ingestion and inhalation

4. Anabolism is a metabolic process that
   a. breaks large molecules into smaller ones.
   b. combines small molecules into larger ones.
   c. distributes oxygen evenly throughout the body.
   d. consumes protein molecules.

5. Which of the following is NOT an accessory organ of the digestive system?
   a. liver
   b. pancreas
   c. gall bladder
   d. urinary bladder

6. The chief function of the colon is to
   a. absorb water from undigested waste.
   b. produce sugars.
   c. absorb protein from undigested waste.
   d. produce carbohydrates.

▶ Answers

1. d. Food molecules must be broken down into their constituent molecules and be small enough to be absorbed, transported, and then reabsorbed by the cells. The cells will then use this energy in the chemical bonds of the broken-down food molecules for cellular respiration.

2. c. Chyme is the slurry that exits in the stomach and enters the small intestine. At this point, some of the foodstuffs in chyme have been broken down (some starch and a lot of the proteins). More digestion takes place as the food moves through the small intestine where many enzymes are present.

3. b. The two metabolic processes that molecules are subjected to at the cellular level are anabolism and catabolism. Cellular respiration is a type of catabolism because a larger molecule (glucose) is broken down to very small molecules (carbon dioxide and water). Anabolism occurs when the cell produces proteins from the free amino acids resulting from the breakdown of proteins in the digestive system.

4. b. Anabolism combines smaller molecules into larger ones.

5. d. The urinary bladder is part of the excretory system.

6. a. The absorption of water from undigested food occurs in the colon.

▶ In Short

To sustain themselves, living organisms must consume organic matter (food). The biochemical reactions of metabolism use this food as energy and occur at the cellular level. Two main types of reactions exist: anabolism and catabolism.

Before the cells can use food for energy, the large molecules we eat must be broken down into smaller molecules that can be absorbed by the body and then distributed to the cells in a usable form. It is the job of the digestive system to break down foodstuffs using chemical and mechanical processes.

LESSON

12 ▶ Structure and Support: The Skeletal System

The skeletal systems of organisms work with the muscles to allow the movement of body parts and the locomotion of the whole organism. They also protect the soft internal organs from injury. The skeletal system also acts as a repository of minerals used in various aspects of metabolism. In vertebrates, the interiors of bones in the skeletal system are responsible for producing blood cells. Skeletal systems appear in arthropods (insects and crustaceans) and vertebrates (birds, fish, reptiles, and mammals). In arthropods, the skeletal system is an *exoskeleton*, and in vertebrates, the skeletal system is an *endoskeleton*.

▶ Vertebrates and Invertebrates

Earlier, when classifying animals, it was mentioned that we separate multicelled animals into two overall, large groups. Those two groups are the vertebrates (those animals with backbones) and the invertebrates (those without backbones). Many invertebrates have no internal skeleton, but they have what is called an *exoskeleton,* which is a hard outer coating. Insects, crabs, and lobsters all have exoskeletons. Muscles can attach to the exoskeleton, which acts as protective body armor. The disadvantage to an exoskeleton is that it limits the organism's growth. Many invertebrates have worked around this problem by molting (or shedding) their exoskeletons at various stages in their life cycles so that they can grow their bodies and then grow a new exoskeleton.

In vertebrate animals, the skeleton is internal (an endoskeleton) and has evolved structures called *vertebrae,* which are hard, bony projections surrounding the spinal cord. This vertebral column is commonly known as the backbone. Although the exoskeleton of invertebrates is dead, excreted tissue (such as hair and nails), the endoskeleton of vertebrates is composed of living tissue that is known as the *skeletal system.* The cells that make up the skeletal system are called *osteocytes,* and they associate together to form connective tissue. This connective tissue, along with cartilage tissue (another type of connective tissue), comprises the skeletal system. Because the skeletal system is alive, it can grow with the organism and molting is not necessary.

The Skeletal System

The *skeleton* is the chief structural system, which, along with the skin, provides form and shape to the body. In human beings, the skeletal system has 206 bones, most of which are in the hands and feet. The bones of the skeletal system are rigid, but the whole system is flexible because of the joints where bones are joined.

This system of bones is highly coordinated with the muscular system. The nervous system is responsible for the coordination necessary for such actions as painting fine detail in a picture or participating in an Olympic decathlon. The skeletal system is a wonderful example of how specialized tissues, collected together into several different organ systems, are further organized into cooperative groups of interacting systems. The muscular and skeletal systems are so closely linked that they are often referred to as one large system called the *musculoskeletal system.*

Bones Are Alive

When you see a bone, it certainly doesn't look alive. However, *bones* are actually living tissue with cells that require food molecules for cellular metabolism and that are served by the circulatory system. Small canals in the bone tissue allow the blood vessels to enter the interior of bones where a soft, pulpy tissue called *marrow* exists. Bone marrow is the tissue that produces blood cells and platelets (the clotting factors of the blood).

Because they are alive, bones can grow. They are initially formed from cartilage or other connective tissue. As the organism grows, much of this connective tissue is replaced with calcium phosphate mineral formations. At the ends of long bones in the arms and legs are growth plates that still consist of cartilage even in teenagers and some young adults. As new cartilage is made, the older part of the growth plate will ossify (turn to bone), lengthening the bone. In adulthood, this growth of new cartilage at the ends of the growth plates stops, and the bones are no longer able to grow longer. However, bone tissue is constantly being broken down and reformed. Calcium is deposited and removed from the reservoir stored in the bones. Thus, bones are not static; they are very much alive.

Joints

A *joint* is the place where two bones come together, and special connective tissues at the joint prevent the bones from damaging each other. Joints hold bones in place but allow them to be far enough apart for movement. Joints can be freely movable (such as the elbow or knee), slightly movable (such as the vertebrae in the back), or immovable (such as the joints that join the bones of the skull together).

But What about Plants?

Plants also need to support their tissues and give shape to their bodies. However, they do not do so with a skeletal system. Nonvascular plants do not have a great need for support because they don't grow very tall, but vascular plants need to be supported by rigid tissue. The cells that make up the vascular tissue of plants form a continuous system of tubes running from the roots through the stems and to the leaves. Water and nutrients flow to the leaves through vascular tissue called *xylem,* where they are used in the process of photosynthesis. Following that process, the products of photosynthesis then flow through vascular tissue called *phloem* back down to the roots.

▶ Practice

1. Which of the following is NOT a function of the skeletal system in animals?
   a. storehouse of minerals
   b. storehouse of oils
   c. protection of internal organs
   d. produce red blood cells

2. Which of the following is NOT true of bones?
   a. They are alive.
   b. They contain marrow, which produces white blood cells.
   c. They are present in vertebrates.
   d. They directly touch each other at a joint.

3. Xylem and phloem are plant tissues that
   a. produce sugar molecules and oxygen.
   b. transport water and nutrients throughout the plant.
   c. contain chloroplasts.
   d. produce seeds.

4. The products of photosynthesis in the leaves flow to the roots through vascular tissue called
   a. phloem.
   b. xylem.
   c. meristem.
   d. angiosperm.

5. Which of the following animals does NOT have an exoskeleton?
   a. insects
   b. crabs
   c. lobsters
   d. earthworms

6. What type of tissue is found at joints and protects bones from rubbing against each other and becoming damaged?
   a. contractile
   b. connective
   c. conductive
   d. catabolic

▶ Answers

1. **b.** The skeletal system does not store oils, but the other responses are true skeletal system functions.
2. **d.** Bones do not directly touch each other at joints; they are close enough to allow for support and movement but are still separated by connective tissue.
3. **b.** The transport of water and nutrients between the leaves and roots happens through the xylem and phloem tissues. These tissues also lend support to the plant.
4. **a.** phloem
5. **d.** earthworms
6. **b.** connective

▶ In Short

The skeleton is the chief structural system, which, along with the skin, provides form and shape to the body. In human beings, the skeletal system has 206 bones, most of which are found in the hands and feet. The bones of the skeletal system are rigid, but the whole system is flexible because of the joints where bones are joined. This system of bones is also highly coordinated with the muscular system. Bones are actually living tissue with cells that require food molecules for cellular metabolism and that are served by the circulatory system. Plants do not have skeletal systems, but they do have a need for support. Nonvascular plants rely on the rigid walls of their cells because they don't grow very tall. Vascular plants, however, need to be supported by rigid tissue and have a system of tubes for transporting water and nutrients throughout the plant body, even to very great heights.

13 ▶ Movement: The Muscular System

To move a body part or the whole body, an organism needs to use the muscular system (in conjunction with the skeletal system). The nervous system controls the three types of muscle tissue found in the body. Sometimes, this is done with our conscious control, and sometimes, it is done automatically without our control.

▶ Three Types of Muscle Tissue

All muscle tissue consists of cells that have evolved to specialize in contracting, yet even with this common function, the three types of muscular tissue have different structures. *Skeletal* (or *striated*) muscle tissue is consciously controlled by the central nervous system. This type of tissue is attached to the bones, and when it contracts, it moves them. Skeletal tissue also forms the visible muscles and much of the body mass. The second type of muscle tissue is called *smooth,* and it is usually not under conscious control. Smooth tissue is usually found in the internal organs, especially the intestinal tract and in the walls of blood vessels. The third type of muscle tissue is called *cardiac,* and it is found only in the heart. This type of muscle tissue is so specialized to contract that it will continue to do so even without stimulation from the nervous system (although it will be a series of uncoordinated contractions that aren't very good at moving blood around the body). Isolated heart cells in a dish will continue to contract on their own until oxygen or nutrient sources are used up.

Antagonistic Pairs

Muscles *only* contract; they do not expand. Muscles are grouped in pairs, often in what are called *antagonistic pairs,* because they are arranged in opposition to each other. Each member of the pair is able to contract, but it doesn't contract at the same time. When one muscle of the pair contracts, the attached joint will move and the bone involved will also move. The other muscle in the pair will lengthen because it is being stretched, not because it is expanding. When the limb gets moved back to its original position, the muscle that contracted will now lengthen as its antagonistic partner contracts.

As an example, when you bring your fist to your shoulder in the classic "making a muscle" bodybuilder pose, you are contracting the biceps muscle on the upper inside of your arm. This muscle moves the elbow joint and raises your lower arm. The muscle opposite the biceps, called the *triceps,* is on the backside of your arm. While the biceps contracts, the triceps is stretched, which is its relaxed state. When you want to lower your arm, the triceps will contract and the biceps will relax, moving the elbow joint in the opposite direction. The biceps and triceps act as an antagonistic muscle pair.

▶ How Do Muscles Work?

In order for muscles to contract, two muscle proteins are necessary: *actin* and *myosin.* Muscle contraction begins when a nerve impulse causes the release of a chemical, called a *neurotransmitter,* that activates the muscle cells and stimulates them to contract. Muscle contraction is explained as the interaction of thick bands of myosin and thin bands of actin. The thick myosin filaments have small knob-like projections that grab onto the thin actin filaments. As these knobs move slightly, they pull the actin filaments, which slide alongside the myosin filaments. This has the effect of shortening the muscle and thus causing a contraction.

Actin and myosin are not muscles themselves; they are protein molecules that literally grab onto each other and bend or move so that one slides past the other. This is done in roughly the same way you might climb a knotted rope by grabbing a knot and pulling your body up to the next knot, then grabbing onto the next and pulling again.

Muscles are not directly attached to bone. Connective tissue known as *tendons* forms a link between them (whereas *ligaments* form a link between two bones). The contraction of a muscle results in the exertion of force upon the tendon, which then pulls the bone to which it is attached. All this movement is coordinated by the central nervous system and results in some very graceful movement, as well as the everyday, but still amazing, ability to walk from one place to another.

▶ How Do Single-Celled Animals Move?

One-celled organisms, such as protists or even sperm cells, within otherwise multicellular animals have the ability to move from place to place. This kind of movement can be accomplished in three different ways. In the case of amoeba, which are one-celled formless blobs of protoplasm, they creep along by extending a portion of themselves and then flowing into that por-

Plants don't move, so are they alive? As previous chapters have discussed, plants are very much alive yet immobile, but they do engage in lots of other movements. At the cellular level, molecules move across the cell membrane, and at the macroscopic level their tissues move frequently in the wind. To move to a new territory, plants must produce seeds or spores, which wind, water, or animals then easily move from place to place.

tion. Other organisms use *cilia*, which are tiny hair-like projections from the cell membrane that can wave about and cause the cell to move. The third way is to use a *flagellum*, which is a tail-like projection that whips around or spins to move the organism.

▶ Practice

1. What are the three types of muscle cells?
   a. cardiac, synaptic, skeletal
   b. cardiac, autonomic, smooth
   c. skeletal, cardiac, smooth
   d. smooth, cardiac, spinal

2. Which of the following is NOT true about skeletal muscles?
   a. They expand.
   b. They contract.
   c. They operate in antagonistic pairs.
   d. They are also known as striated muscles.

3. What are the two protein molecules responsible for the contraction of muscles?
   a. pepsin and insulin
   b. myosin and pepsin
   c. hemoglobin and insulin
   d. myosin and actin

4. When thinking about plant movement, why is it important for plants to produce seeds and spores?
   a. to guarantee survival of the sporophyte generation
   b. to have animals transport the seeds and spores to new locations because plants are rooted
   c. to feed animals
   d. to assist in the process of photosynthesis

5. Peristalsis is a process performed by which type of muscle tissue?
   a. catabolic
   b. cardiac
   c. smooth
   d. skeletal

▶ Answers

1. c. These are the three types of muscle cells. Skeletal cells are also called striated and are involved in moving the bones at joints; cardiac muscles are found only in the heart; and smooth muscles are found in the digestive system and are involved in moving food by peristalsis.

2. a. Skeletal muscles work in antagonistic pairs (such as your biceps at the front of your upper arm and your triceps in the back) and only contract. One muscle in a pair contracts to move the limb, and then the opposing (antagonistic) muscle contracts to pull the limb back into its original position.

3. d. Myosin and actin are the two proteins that work in conjunction to cause muscle contraction.

4. b. Because plants are rooted and stationary, they are unable to move from place to place. One way in which plants establish themselves in a new territory is to rely upon animals (or wind or water) to transport seeds and spores that will germinate and develop into a new adult plant.

5. c. A smooth muscle performs peristalsis or rhythmic contractions to push foodstuffs along the length of the intestinal tract.

▶ In Short

All muscle tissue consists of cells that have evolved to specialize in contracting, yet even with this common function, the three types of muscular tissue have different structures. Skeletal (or striated) muscle tissue is consciously controlled by the central nervous system. The second type is called smooth and is usually not under conscious control. The third type is called cardiac and is found only in the heart. Muscles *only* contract; they do not expand. They work in antagonistic pairs to move a joint or by using peristaltic, wave-like movement in the intestinal tract.

One-celled organisms, such as protists or even sperm cells, in otherwise multicellular animals have the ability to move from place to place. They do this in three different ways: by extending portions of their body, by cilia, and or by flagella. Most plants, however, do not relocate or move from place to place, but they engage in lots of other movements.

14 ▶ Gas Exchange: The Respiratory System

In an earlier lesson, we discussed cellular respiration, which is a part of metabolism and is a set of chemical reactions. In this lesson on the respiratory system, we examine the physical process of exchanging gases between our bodies and the atmosphere—in other words, breathing. It is important for organisms to get rid of waste gases and to absorb helpful gases necessary for the chemical processes of metabolism.

▶ When Is Respiration Not Breathing?

The word respiration is used in two different but related ways in biology. In one sense, respiration means the act of bringing air into the lungs and expelling waste gases. We call this form of respiration *breathing*. However, the chemical reactions of metabolism partly contain a set of reactions that use enzymes and oxygen to burn food molecules and release the energy of their bonds. This process is more specifically known as *cellular aerobic respiration* (or *anaerobic* when no oxygen is present). Sometimes, the two types of respiration are differentiated by being *internal* (cellular respiration) and *external* (the act of breathing). Here, we are talking about the process of breathing, which has the important function of allowing for the exchange of gases.

Who Respires?

All organisms, even single-celled ones, must perform cellular respiration (either aerobically or anaerobically) during metabolism to obtain necessary energy to support life functions. Because single-celled animals are small, they have no need of a respiratory system to help them breathe. They can simply exchange gases across their cell membranes. However, multicellular animals are too large to rely only upon diffusion for gas exchange. They must also have specialized tissues to perform this function.

▶ The Respiratory System

The vertebrate respiratory system can essentially be divided into two parts, the part that conducts air and the gas exchange portion. The series of conducting tubes brings air into the gas exchange portion. Breathing involves *inhalation* (the taking in of air) and *exhalation* (the releasing of air).

Conduction of Air

Organisms breathe through their nose or mouth, and air enters the upper part of the throat or the *pharynx*. The next point of note is the *larynx* or what is called the Adam's apple on the inside of the throat. The larynx is also known as the voice box because the cartilage here changes shape to help form the sounds of speech. Inhaled air next passes into the *trachea*, which is a tube in the center of the chest. Within the chest, the trachea branches into two *bronchi*. Each bronchus leads to a lung. Once inside the lung, the bronchus branches repeatedly into small tubes called *bronchioles*. Bronchiole tubes then lead to a microscopic sac-like structure called an *alveolus* (plural is *alveoli*). The alveoli are the site of the second function of the respiratory system: gas exchange.

Gas Exchange

The lung provides a moist and warm surface for gas exchange. Each lung has over two million alveoli, which provide a huge surface area for gas exchange, equal to about 800 square feet. In contrast, the skin surface area of your body is only ten square feet. All of that is packed within each of your lungs, which really only have a relatively small volume if it weren't for all of the alveoli. So again we see the power of branching and folding to increase surface area in relation to volume.

The alveolus is a small sac surrounded by blood vessels. The walls of the sac and the walls of the surrounding blood vessels are very thin, allowing for diffusion of gases in either direction. The hemoglobin of the red blood cells has a greater affinity for oxygen than it does for carbon dioxide. Thus, when the blood stream interfaces with the outside air in the alveolus, oxygen diffuses into the blood and carbon dioxide diffuses into the sac of the alveolus, to be exhaled with the next breath. Blood entering the lungs is low in oxygen and high in carbon dioxide because of cellular respiration (metabolism), whereas air entering the lungs from the atmosphere is high in oxygen and low in carbon dioxide. Thus, the alveoli contain a high concentration of oxygen and a low carbon dioxide concentration. However, the blood in the blood vessels lining the alveoli has exactly the opposite condition, so the two gases flow in opposite directions. This is the gas exchange of respiration. The blood in the blood vessels lining the alveoli has a high oxygen concentration and flows out of the lungs to go to the rest of the body.

Plants exchange gas as well. Single-celled plants, like their animal counterparts, simply exchange gases through the cell membranes. Multicellular plants must develop specialized tissues. The plant uses pores on the leaf surface, called *stomata*, to exchange gases with the atmosphere.

What Happens in the Body's Cells?

Once the newly oxygenated blood leaves the lungs, it is distributed throughout the body to every cell. Each cell engages in cellular respiration (metabolism), thus using up oxygen and producing carbon dioxide. Inside the cell is thus a high concentration of carbon dioxide, but in the blood and surrounding fluid outside the cell, the concentration of carbon dioxide is low. So, again, a gas exchange occurs where oxygen flows from a high concentration outside the cell to the low-concentration side on the inside of the cell. Carbon dioxide flows in the opposite direction. The blood is now high in carbon dioxide and makes its way back to the lungs for more gas exchange with atmospheric air that has been breathed in and conducted to the lungs.

▶ Practice

1. In the conduction of air through the respiratory system, which of the following is the correct order?
   a. pharynx, larynx, alveoli, trachea, bronchus, bronchioles
   b. alveoli, bronchioles, bronchus, trachea, larynx, pharynx
   c. pharynx, larynx, trachea, bronchus, bronchioles, alveoli
   d. bronchus, bronchioles, alveoli, pharynx, larynx, trachea

2. Each alveolus in the lungs is covered by tiny blood vessels to perform which of these functions?
   a. excretion of urine
   b. gas exchange
   c. blood production
   d. enzymatic digestion

3. The pores on a plant leaf that allow for gas exchange are called
   a. alveoli.
   b. cell pores.
   c. membrane gaps.
   d. stomata.

4. During gas exchange at a cell, which of the following is occurring?
   a. Oxygen is flowing from a low concentration inside the cell to a high concentration outside the cell.
   b. Oxygen is flowing from a high concentration in the red blood cells to a low concentration inside the body cell.
   c. Carbon dioxide is moving from the red blood cells into the body cells.
   d. Carbon dioxide is flowing from a low concentration outside the cells to a high concentration inside the cells.

5. The lungs are very efficient at gas exchange because they have a
   a. high mass.
   b. low volume.
   c. high surface-area-to-volume ratio.
   d. low surface-area-to-volume ratio.

▶ Answers

1. c. Air enters through the nose or mouth, the pharynx is at the upper part of the throat, and the larynx is very close to the top of the throat. The tube leading through the chest to the lungs is the trachea, which branches into two bronchi. Each bronchus further branches into bronchioles, which lead directly to the alveoli.

2. b. The interface between the alveoli, which contain air, and the tiny circulatory vessels, which contain blood, is very thin. Oxygen flows out of the aveoli and into the circulation, while carbon dioxide flows out of the circulation and into the alveoli where it is excreted by exhalation.

3. d. Stomata are small openings on the leaf surface that allow for gas exchange.

4. b. Oxygen flows from a high concentration (in the red blood cells) to a low concentration (in the body cells); carbon dioxide flows in the opposite direction.

5. c. In a relatively small volume, the lungs contain a huge surface area because of the branching bronchioles, which eventually end in millions of alveoli.

▶ In Short

The word respiration is used in two different but related ways in biology. In one sense, respiration means the act of bringing air into the lungs and expelling waste gases. We call this form of respiration breathing. However, the chemical reactions of metabolism partly contain a set of reactions that use enzymes and oxygen to burn food molecules and release the energy of their bonds. This process is more specifically known as cellular aerobic respiration (or anaerobic when no oxygen is present). All organisms, even single-celled ones, must perform cellular respiration (either aerobically or anaerobically) during metabolism to obtain necessary energy to support life functions.

The vertebrate respiratory system contains two parts, the part that conducts air and the gas exchange portion. The trachea, bronchus, and brochials form the tube that conducts air from the mouth and nose into the lungs. The alveoli are the site of gas exchange within the lungs.

Plants have a gas exchange process as well. Single-celled plants, like their animal counterparts, simply exchange gases through the cell membranes. Multicellular plants must develop specialized tissues, and the plants use pores on the leaf surface, called stomata, to exchange gases with the atmosphere.

15 ▶ Circulation: The Cardiovascular System

The cells in living organisms need to have nutrients transported to them and waste products removed. In single-celled organisms, there isn't much need for the transport of nutrients and wastes because the organism can diffuse these substances to and from the environment directly through the cell membrane. In larger multicelled organisms, this is not possible, so instead, these substances diffuse into and out of the circulatory system. In animals, this system is based on a liquid suspension of specialized cells. We call the liquid *plasma,* and the cells are called *blood cells*. The two make up what we call *blood*. In plants, this transport system is based on the special properties of water, not blood.

▶ The Parts of the Cardiovascular System

The cardiovascular system, sometimes also called the circulatory system, has three main parts. From the name, we can see two of those parts mentioned. "Cardio" refers to the heart, which is the pump in the system. "Vascular" refers to vessels, specifically the blood vessels that provide a route for fluids in the system. The third component is a very specialized fluid called *blood* that serves as the means of transport for nutrients and oxygen, as well as wastes.

- Oxygen from the lungs to the body's cells
- Carbon dioxide from the body's cells to the lungs
- Nutrients from the digestive system to the cells
- Waste products other than carbon dioxide to the liver and kidneys
- Hormones and other messenger chemicals from the glands and organs of their production to the body's cells

The Four-Chambered Heart

In vertebrate animals, the heart has evolved to have four chambers that can fill with blood, which is then squeezed out by the muscular walls of the heart. The four chambers are very important for keeping blood that contains wastes from mixing with fresh blood. In the circulatory system, the vessels that take blood to the heart are called *veins,* and the vessels that take blood away from the heart are called *arteries.* The *superior vena cava* is a vein that brings the blood from the body into the top right chamber called the *right atrium.* This atrium is separated from the chamber below it by a valve and is separated from the chamber next to it by a muscle wall. Blood flows through the valve when the heart relaxes after a beat from the right atrium into the chamber below called the *right ventricle.* The right ventricle is muscular enough to send the blood through the pulmonary arteries to the lungs.

Blood is refreshed in the lungs and then flows through the pulmonary veins back to the upper part of the heart, but this time, it enters on the left side into the *left atrium.* This atrium is again separated from the ventricle below by a valve. When this valve opens during the relaxed phase of the heart, blood flows into the left ventricle. This chamber is the largest and has the strongest muscular wall so that it can propel blood into the *aorta,* which is the largest artery, leading away from the heart to the rest of the body.

Arteries branch off from the aorta and travel to all parts of the body. As you trace a vessel through the body, it continues to branch and get smaller until it becomes what we call an *arteriole.* Arterioles lead to very small beds of tiny blood vessels called *capillaries.* These capillary beds are where the exchange of nutrients, gases, and wastes occurs. As blood that now contains wastes leaves the capillary beds, it enters small vessels called *venules.* These course their way through the body back to the heart and, on the way, become larger veins, which eventually empty into the large vena cava vein that empties into the heart.

Earlier we said that blood leaving the heart travels in vessels called arteries. For the most part, this means that the blood is fresh and oxygenated because it is to be distributed to the rest of the body. However, if you read closely, you will notice that the vessels leaving the heart and heading toward the lungs are called arteries as well (the pulmonary arteries), but they contain deoxygenated, nonfresh blood. So it is always true that blood leaving the heart travels in arteries, but it is not always true that this is fresh blood. The reverse is true for veins, which usually carry nonfresh blood, except for the pulmonary veins, which enter the heart from the lungs and carry fresh, oxygenated blood.

The Composition of Blood

The "vital fluid" and the "river of life" are phrases used to describe blood. It earns these important descriptors because it is the blood that helps regulate our internal environment and keep us in a relatively constant state known as *homeostasis*. Blood transports and mixes elements up, making it possible for all the organs to contribute to maintaining homeostasis. Blood is not strictly a fluid but is better thought of as a suspension. Suspensions are fluids containing particles suspended inside them. Blood has two components: the liquid portion called plasma and the cells suspended throughout. The cells come in three major types: the *red blood cells*, the *white blood cells*, and the cellular fragments called *platelets*.

Plasma is mostly water in which some substances such as proteins, hormones, and nutrients (glucose sugar, vitamins, amino acids, and fats) are dissolved. Gases (carbon dioxide and oxygen), salts (of calcium, chloride, and potassium), and wastes other than carbon dioxide are also dissolved in blood. The red blood cells contain a protein called *hemoglobin*. The hemoglobin molecule has an atom of iron contained within its structure. The hemoglobin molecule binds to oxygen and carbon dioxide, and thus provides the mechanism by which the red blood cells can carry these gases around the body. The white blood cells come in many specialized forms and are used in the immune system to fight invading organisms and keep us from getting diseases. The platelets release substances at the site of a wound that start the blood-clotting reaction.

▶ Practice

1. Which of the following is NOT one of the chambers in the four-chambered vertebrate heart?
   a. right atrium
   b. right ventricle
   c. left alveolar
   d. left ventricle

2. Which of the following is true about blood flow in the four-chambered vertebrate heart circulatory system?
   a. Blood in the pulmonary vein is oxygenated.
   b. Blood in the pulmonary artery is oxygenated.
   c. Blood in the aorta is not oxygenated.
   d. Blood in the vena cava is oxygenated.

3. Which of the following two items are the major components of blood?
   a. proteins and lipids
   b. plasma and cells
   c. proteins and platelets
   d. cells and lipids

4. Platelets perform which of the following functions?
   a. blood clotting
   b. carrying oxygen
   c. carrying carbon dioxide
   d. disease protection

5. Capillary beds occur between
   a. arteries and veins.
   b. aortas and vena cavas.
   c. arterioles and venules.
   d. atria and ventricles.

6. Red blood cells perform which of the following functions?
   a. blood clotting
   b. carrying oxygen
   c. disease protection
   d. wound healing

▶ Answers

1. c. The four-chambered vertebrate heart is made up of the right and left ventricles and the right and left atria. The atria receive blood from the body (the vena cava) and the lungs (the pulmonary vein). The ventricles push blood out of the heart to the body (the aorta) or the lungs (the pulmonary artery).

2. a. Remember that all veins carry blood toward the heart and all arteries carry blood away from the heart. Thus, usually arteries (like the aorta) will be carrying oxygenated blood, and veins (like the vena cava) will be carrying blood that is not oxygenated. However, in the heart-to-lung part of the system, the vessel carrying blood away from the heart and toward the lungs is an artery (the pulmonary artery), but it is carrying blood that is not oxygenated because that's why it's going to the lung (to become oxygenated). Likewise, the vessel carrying blood from the lungs to the heart (the pulmonary vein) is carrying blood that has been oxygenated.

3. b. Blood is a suspension of the fluid we call plasma and the cells that are suspended throughout it. The cells are the red and white blood cells and the platelets.

4. a. Platelets aid in the clotting of blood to seal off a wound and prevent blood loss or infection.

5. c. Capillary beds are between the very small arteries called arterioles and the very small veins called venules. Capillary beds are the site of gas exchange in the circulatory system.

6. b. Red blood cells carry oxygen, but they also carry carbon dioxide.

▶ In Short

The cardiovascular system, sometimes also called the circulatory system, has three main parts. From the name, we can see two of those parts mentioned. "Cardio" refers to the heart, which is the pump in the system. "Vascular" refers to vessels, specifically the blood vessels that provide a route for fluids in the system. The third component is a very specialized fluid called blood that serves as the means of transport for nutrients and oxygen, as well as wastes. Arteries lead blood away from the heart, and veins return blood toward the heart. Capillary beds are the site of exchange for gases, nutrients, and wastes. Blood is a special fluid with red and white cells and platelets suspended in it.

16 ▶ Filtration and Excretion: The Renal System

The chemical reactions of metabolism that occur in the cells of organisms produce waste substances that must be excreted. One-celled organisms can excrete toxic substances by diffusion through their cell membranes or by using specialized organelles called *vacuoles*, whereas multicellular organisms have developed special organ systems to accomplish the same task. The circulatory and excretory systems work together to eliminate metabolic wastes.

▶ Homeostasis

All organisms try to live in a favorable environment, but even such an environment will have conditions that fluctuate over time. Organisms must be able to respond to these changes and yet still maintain a relatively constant internal environment within their bodies. For instance, they must maintain a balance of water, temperature, and salt concentration. The series of physical and chemical processes that work to maintain an internal equilibrium is called *homeostasis*. We first mentioned homeostasis in the circulatory system lesson. The circulatory system and the filtration/excretion system work very closely together to help maintain homeostasis.

► Filtration and Excretion

When you eat food, some of it is indigestible and must be eliminated by the digestive tract. However, the digestible part is broken down and eventually absorbed as very small molecules. These molecules are transported to the cells by the blood. The cells then carry out the biochemical reactions of metabolism, which results in wastes such as carbon dioxide. The carbon dioxide is carried by the blood to the lungs where it is exhaled, but other wastes are produced during cellular metabolism besides carbon dioxide. For the most part, these wastes cannot be eliminated in the lungs. Instead, they must be filtered out of the blood and then excreted.

The Kidneys as Filters

The blood delivers wastes such as ammonia, which comes from the metabolism of amino acids in cells, to the liver where they are converted into *urea*. The blood then carries the urea to the organs in the lower back called the *kidneys*. The kidneys are bean-shaped (they look very much like a kidney bean, in fact!) and are about the size of your fist. They are part of the renal system, which also includes the *ureters* and *urethra*, two tubes that carry the liquid wastes out of the body. The *urinary bladder*, a holding place for urine, is also part of this system.

The kidneys are sophisticated filters. They are able to take urea, which is less toxic than ammonia but still not well tolerated in high concentrations, and convert it into urine, which is very soluble in water and can be excreted. The kidneys also regulate the amount of water that is used in this process in order to prevent body dehydration. Kidneys also maintain proper levels of a number of substances in the body (including sodium, potassium, chloride, calcium, glucose sugar, and amino acids) by reabsorbing them from urine before it is excreted. The kidneys also help maintain blood pressure and the acidity (pH) level of the blood. It is obvious that the kidneys are important regulators and maintainers of bodily homeostasis.

How Does a Kidney Work?

In each kidney are at least a million individual units called *nephrons*. Functionally, nephrons are similar to the alveoli in the lungs. The alveoli are structured to function as gas exchange interfaces, whereas the kidney nephrons are structured to function as fluid interchange points.

Each nephron consists of a bed of capillaries with thin walls surrounded by a tube structure called *Bowman's capsule*. Filtration of the blood occurs for water, nutrients, and wastes through the capillaries into the Bowman's capsule. Most of the water and nutrients are reabsorbed right away. This concentrates the wastes in the fluid inside the Bowman's capsule tubules. We now call this fluid urine.

The tubules leading away from Bowman's capsule eventually arrive at the collecting duct where even more water may be absorbed. The collecting duct leads to the interior of the kidney where urine collects and flows into the ureters, which take it to the urinary bladder. Urine will collect in the urinary bladder until the urge to urinate is strong enough that the urine is expelled from the body through the urethra.

Monitoring Water Levels

Part of what the kidneys do is regulate the amount of water that circulates in the bloodstream. If the brain detects low levels of water in the blood, then more antidiuretic hormone (ADH) is released. As its name implies, it causes the kidneys to reabsorb water into the bloodstream, thus concentrating the urine and preserving water for the body.

The brain is very good at keeping a balance on many interrelated factors. Our nervous system responds to sensors in the body that keep track of blood sugar, blood pressure, blood carbon dioxide, blood oxygen, blood dissolved salts, and so on. Lack of water affects all these values, which is how the body detects it.

When you drink too much alcohol, you usually urinate more often. This is because alcohol inhibits the action of the ADH signal from the brain. Thus, nothing tells the kidneys to conserve water.

▶ Practice

1. The kidneys are responsible for filtering which of the following from the blood?
  a. undigested food
  b. metabolic wastes
  c. blood cells
  d. platelets

2. The kidneys function as blood filters. Which of the following is NOT another function of the kidneys?
  a. regulating pH (acidity) of blood
  b. regulating blood pressure
  c. assisting in the maintenance of homeostasis
  d. regulating hormone release

3. The nephron of the kidney produces
  a. urine.
  b. ammonia.
  c. nucleic acids.
  d. amino acids.

4. Wastes concentrated in the tubules of Bowman's capsule are called
  a. urine.
  b. salts.
  c. nucleic acids.
  d. amino acids.

5. Drinking alcohol causes more urination because it
  a. adds too much water to the body.
  b. accelerates the action of antidiuretic hormone.
  c. decreases the action of antidiuretic hormone.
  d. increases water reabsorption.

► Answers

1. b. The digestive system removes undigested food, and the kidneys remove the waste products of all the biochemical reactions that make up the metabolism, especially the wastes from protein breakdown.

2. d. The regulation of hormone release is really the function mostly of a region of the brain. The kidneys do perform the other functions listed as choices.

3. a. By filtering the blood and removing wastes, the nephrons of the kidneys produce a liquid called urine.

4. a. Urine is the name of the waste fluid in the tubules of Bowman's capsule.

5. c. Alcohol inhibits the action of the antidiuretic hormone, which causes more urine to be produced and a greater loss of water than normal.

► In Short

The series of physical and chemical processes that work to maintain an internal equilibrium is called homeostasis. The circulatory system and the filtration/excretion system work very closely together to help maintain homeostasis, and wastes other than carbon dioxide are produced during cellular metabolism. For the most part, these wastes cannot be eliminated in the lungs, and instead, they must be filtered out of the blood by the kidneys and then be excreted.

The kidneys are sophisticated filters. They are able to take urea—which is less toxic than ammonia but still not well tolerated in high concentrations—and convert it to urine, which is very soluble in water and can be excreted. The quantity of water in the body is tightly controlled, and the kidneys play an important role in that necessary function. The amount of water in the blood is controlled in what is called a negative feedback loop.

Irritability and Responses to the Environment: The Nervous System

As we mentioned earlier, interaction with the environment is a unique characteristic of life. The term we use to describe the response of an organism to a change in its surroundings is *irritability*. You can think of this in terms of a stimulus (meaning a change in the surroundings), which irritates an organism and triggers a response. Both plants and animals can respond to an environmental stimulus. In multicelled animals, we have what is known as a nervous system. Plants do not have nervous systems, but they do have cellular receptors that respond to many environmental stimuli.

▶ Interacting with the Environment

The nervous system of multicelled, vertebrate animals is very sophisticated and able to respond to many external and internal stimuli. Think of a dog who sees a squirrel in the yard. He will receive the visual stimulus through his eyes, which will send a signal to his brain. The brain then remembers that a squirrel is something fun to chase and sends signals to the dog's leg muscles. The dog will run and probably not catch the squirrel, but he will still use his nose to smell the squirrel's scent. After running hard, the dog may be breathing hard and panting, with the breathing muscles also controlled by the nervous system. Having missed the squirrel, the dog may realize he is hungry and the brain will send signals to the stomach and the digestive system. This simple example shows the many necessary interactions the nervous system controls.

Stimulus and Response

In another of the body's cooperative efforts, the nervous system often works in conjunction with the muscular system (as well as all other organ systems). When something causes a change in the environment, the nervous system detects this. Usually, some sort of processing of this information takes place, and a signal is sent out in response. The response is usually to take some action. The action could be the movement of a muscle, the secretion of a substance by a gland, some action in the digestive system, or some regulatory function such as signaling the kidneys to absorb more or less water. The nervous system is built upon cells called *neurons*.

The Neuron

The functional unit of the nervous system is the neuron, a cell with structures specialized in transmitting electrical impulses. A neuron must be able to receive information from internal or external sources, integrate the signal (especially if from multiple sources), send that signal to other parts of the body that may be far away, and then deliver that message to another neuron, gland, or muscle.

In multicelled vertebrates, neurons have four regions. The *dendrites* are the tree-branch-like extensions at one end of the neuron that receive signals from other neurons. The *cell body* of the neuron is where cellular functions take place (just like in any other cell) and where the signal(s) is (are) integrated. The *axon* is a long extension from the cell body, along which the nerve impulse is sent. Some axons are several feet in length. The final region of the neuron is the *synaptic terminal.* This is the very end of the axon and consists of several tiny swellings that contain a chemical substance called a *neurotransmitter.*

A nerve signal reaches the synaptic terminal and causes the neurotransmitter to be released. This chemical messenger then moves across the small space between the neuron and the next neuron (or gland or muscle) called the *synapse.* Once across the synapse, the neurotransmitter is received by the dendrites of another neuron (or the receptors on a gland or muscle). Thus, a signal is transmitted to another neuron in the chain (or to the gland or muscle where action can take place).

The electrical signal produced in the neuron that travels down the axon does not actually cross the tiny synaptic space between neurons (or their target organs). The nervous system relies upon chemical messengers called neurotransmitters to cross the gap. The use of neurotransmitters allows fine-tuning of the signal because different neurotransmitters can be used for different purposes or in different locations.

From One to Many

Although some reflexes involve very few neurons, most of the complex and versatile behavior of vertebrate animals comes from the fact that neurons form many complex connections with other neurons. This complex webbing of many tiny cells reaches its zenith in the vertebrate brain where billions of neurons each make dozens of connections. Collections of individual neurons become what we call *nerves*. The vertebrate nervous system is the name we give to this complex networking of neurons into nerves. The vertebrate nervous system is divided into two major parts, the *central nervous system* and the *peripheral nervous system.*

The central nervous system consists of the brain and spinal cord (contained within the vertebral column or backbone). The brain is a highly specialized organ where neurons have grouped together into many specific areas, each with a specific function. The brain integrates all the signals in the nervous system and thus controls the body. It also acts as a data storage organ by learning and keeping memories. In the higher mammals it is also the seat of the conscious mind.

The peripheral nervous system consists of nerves that connect the central nervous system to the rest of the body. The peripheral nervous system has nerves that connect the brain to each part of the body, including sensory nerves that bring information to the central nervous system and motor nerves that carry signals away from the brain and to the muscles, glands, or organs. The sensory neurons are, in many cases, specialized and have become part of other organs whose function is to sense the internal and external environment. Examples of such organs would be the eyes, ears, touch receptors, and taste buds. The motor portion of the peripheral nervous system is again further divided into the *somatic* and *autonomic nervous systems.*

The somatic nervous system is concerned with motor functions. Its nerves make contact with skeletal muscle and are responsible for controlling movement of all kinds, from fine movements to walking and running.

The autonomic nervous system, also part of the peripheral nervous system, works mostly without our conscious control. It is often responsible for critical life functions such as breathing and heart rate. The autonomic nervous system has two divisions. Nerves from each of these divisions usually make contact with the same organs, but they often have opposite effects. The *sympathetic division* of the autonomic nervous system is responsible for the fight-or-flight response, so it prepares the body for high-energy, stressful situations. The *parasympathetic division* of the autonomic nervous system is responsible for rest and digest functions, so it tends to slow down the body.

Life Without a Nervous System

Plants do not have organized nervous systems or neurons. However, they are expert at using chemical messengers to detect and respond to their environment. Plants make definite responses to light, gravity, touch, and other environmental stimuli. For example, the orientation of a plant toward or away from light, called *phototropism*, is mediated by hormones.

▶ **Practice**

1. What is the functional unit of the nervous system?
   a. the nephron
   b. the nucleus
   c. the neuron
   d. the neutrophil

2. Which of the following IS a part of the central nervous system?
   a. autonomic nerves
   b. sympathetic nerves
   c. peripheral nerves
   d. spinal cord nerves

3. What general type of substance is used at the synapse to carry the nerve signal from one neuron to another?
   a. axon fluid
   b. dendrite fluid
   c. neurotransmitter
   d. hormone

4. Dendrites receive information from
   a. the axon of other neurons.
   b. the dendrites of other neurons.
   c. the cell body of other neurons.
   d. the nucleus of other neurons.

5. Neurotransmitters are released from
   a. axons.
   b. dendrites.
   c. cell bodies.
   d. the nucleus.

6. Which of the following is NOT true about irritability in living organisms?
   a. Plants do not respond to their environment.
   b. Neurons are found in the brain.
   c. Axons can be very long.
   d. Neurons act upon muscles.

▶ Answers

1. c. The neuron is the cell type that produces and transports an electrical signal. Groups of neurons are called nerves. The nephron is the functional unit of the kidney. The nucleus is an organelle within many cells (not prokaryotes like the bacteria) and contains the genetic information. The neutrophil is a type of white blood cell.

2. d. The brain and nerves of the spinal cord are considered to be part of the central nervous system. Autonomic nerves are part of the peripheral nervous system that operate without conscious control, and sympathetic nerves are one type of autonomic nerve. Peripheral nerves control the muscles. All nerves feed back to the brain and spinal cord of the central nervous system.

3. c. Neurotransmitters are the chemical substances produced at the end of the axon of one neuron that float across the synaptic gap to stimulate the dendrites of another axon.

4. a. Neurons are lined up with the axon of one near the dendrite of another.

5. a. Neurotransmitters are released from the end of the axon and cross the synapse to reach the dendrite of another neuron.

6. a. Plants do not have a nervous system, but they have cells that respond to many environmental stimuli.

▶ In Short

The nervous system of multicelled, vertebrate animals is very sophisticated and is able to respond to many external and internal stimuli. The functional unit of the nervous system is the neuron, a cell with structures specialized in transmitting electrical impulses. A neuron must be able to receive information from internal or external sources, integrate the signal (especially if from multiple sources), send that signal to other parts of the body, and then deliver that message to another neuron, gland, or muscle. The electrical signal produced in the neuron, which travels down the axon, does not actually cross the tiny synaptic space between neurons (or their target organs). The nervous system relies upon chemical messengers called neurotransmitters to cross the gap. The vertebrate nervous system is divided into two major parts, the central nervous system and the peripheral nervous system.

18 ▶ Asexual and Sexual Reproduction

Any living organism has a limited life span, but life itself goes on because organisms can create offspring through reproduction. Some organisms can do this without exchanging or combining genetic information with a partner. Thus, all of their offspring will be genetically identical to the parent or clones. Asexual reproduction occurs in all the Kingdoms (Bacteria, Protists, Fungi, Plants, and Animals). Sexual reproduction is when genetic material from one parent is combined with the genetic information from another to yield offspring. These offspring are not identical to either parent. Each parent produces a specialized cell called a *gamete* that contains half of his or her genetic information. The union of these gametes is called *fertilization*.

▶ Asexual Reproduction

All Kingdoms of organisms have representatives that engage in asexual reproduction. Asexual reproduction is an advantage because you do not need to find a partner, and usually, you can reproduce in large numbers very quickly. Sometimes, asexual reproduction is known as *vegetative reproduction*. Organisms that engage in asexual reproduction also usually engage in sexual reproduction with a partner, at least part of the time.

In single-celled organisms such as bacteria and protists, asexual reproduction happens through a process known as *binary fission* (or *bipartition*) in which the cell duplicates certain parts of itself and then splits into two separate but identical cells. Bacteria can do this very fast, even as fast as just 15 or 20 minutes, which is why their populations can increase very quickly. Fungi and some animals, such as coral, reproduce asexually by a process of budding in which an offshoot of their body develops into a complete individual. Multicellular invertebrates such as sea stars can also reproduce asexually by *fragmentation* in which a portion of the organism's body is separated (as in when a sea star loses a limb) and then grows into a whole organism while the original body repairs itself as well. Plants can reproduce asexually by budding or fragmentation when they form tubers, rhizomes, bulbs, and other extensions of their bodies. Plants (and some animals such as jellyfish) also have a major sexual phase of their life cycle, which is part of a process called *alternation of generations*.

Alternation of Generations and Reproduction in Plants

Although asexual reproduction allows plants to reproduce quickly and colonize a large area, most plants still engage in sexual reproduction at least part of the time. A sexually reproducing plant cycles between two distinctly different body types. The first is called the *sporophyte* and the second is called the *gametophyte*. The word "phyte" refers to plant, whereas the prefix "sporo" refers to spores, and the prefix "gameto" refers to gametes (the eggs and sperm).

An adult sporophyte (the form of the plant you are most familiar with), such as a fern, will produce spores (the brown spots on the underside of a fern leaf, for instance). These spores are not gametes because they do not join like an egg and sperm do. Instead, they will be ejected and carried by wind or water to suitable habitats where they will sprout into a gametophyte form of the plant (usually small and not familiar). This gametophyte produces the eggs and sperm that can then join to form a new sporophyte.

Switching from the sporophyte form to the gametophyte form represents the concept of the alternation of generations. This happens in nonflowering plants (like the fern) and also flowering plants,

although here it is less noticeable, and the gametophyte generation is very small and dependent on the sporophyte generation. An oak tree, for instance, is really the sporophyte generation of the plant, while the gametophyte generation is contained within the flowers, which are themselves inconspicuous.

▶ Sexual Reproduction in Animals

Asexual reproduction is an advantage in that you can reproduce quickly and don't need to find a mate. However, when two organisms can mate and reproduce sexually, they have the opportunity to recombine genetic characteristics from both parents. This gives offspring new and often advantageous characteristics that they would not have if they were identical to the single parent they came from.

Sexual reproduction in plants and animals depends on the production of two different gametes or sex cells. Male animals produce the smaller, more mobile gamete known as a *sperm cell*. Females produce the larger, more sedentary gamete known as an *egg cell*. These two gametes must be brought into contact and must fuse and combine their genetic information. When egg and sperm meet, we call this *fertilization*. This can happen externally (especially in an aquatic environment) or internally. Sometimes, external fertilization is done a bit haphazardly. Eggs and sperm are both released into the water, and they must find each other. This type of fertilization, known as *spawning*, is dependent on each gender synchronizing its reproductive cycles to the other. For some fish and amphibians, such as frogs, each gender actually meets and embraces to stimulate the release of each type of gamete, although no internal fertilization takes place.

Internal fertilization is dependent on copulation, a process in which the male deposits sperm cells directly into the reproductive tract of the female. Each gender has developed specialized structures for the delivery and receipt of the sperm cells, as well as for ensuring that the egg cells are fertilized. For land-based species, internal fertilization is critical because a medium-like water cannot be used to transport and support the gametes. The lack of abundant water can also easily dry out the gametes, making them unusable. The important structures in the male and female vertebrate reproductive systems are described in the following table.

MALE STRUCTURE	FUNCTION	FEMALE STRUCTURE	FUNCTION
Testis (plural testes), also called testicles	Produces sperm cells and male hormones	Ovary (plural ovaries)	Produces egg cells and female hormones
Epididymis	Stores sperm cells while they mature	Uterine duct, also called the fallopian tubes	Tube that transports the egg cell to the uterus
Vas deferens	Tube that transports the sperm cells to the urethra	Uterus, also called the womb	Muscular chamber that supports and nourishes the developing fetus
Urethra	Tube that transports sperm from the vas deferens and urine from the urinary bladder, though not at the same time	Cervix	Ring of connective tissue that closes off the lower end of the uterus
Penis	External appendage that contains the urethra and is able to erect and deposit sperm cells into the female reproductive tract	Vagina	A large duct that receives the penis and is where sperm cells are deposited; acts as birth canal when fetus is birthed
Prostate gland	Produces fluids that nourish sperm cells	Labia	External genitalia surrounding the entrance to the vagina

▶ Practice

1. The formation of tubers is an example of what kind of asexual reproduction in plants?
   a. budding
   b. binary fission
   c. bipartition
   d. root zone development

2. The alternation of generations in plants occurs in which of the following ways?
   a. The sporophyte produces eggs and sperm that join and lead to the development of a gametophyte.
   b. The gametophyte produces eggs and sperm that join and lead to the development of a sporophyte.
   c. The gametophyte produces eggs and the sporophyte produces sperm that join to form a new plant.
   d. The sporophyte produces eggs and the gametophyte produces sperm that join to form a new plant.

3. In sexually reproducing vertebrate animals, which pair of structures is similar to one another because they are both responsible for the production of gametes?
   a. oviduct and vas deferens
   b. vagina and penis
   c. ovaries and testes
   d. uterus and prostate gland

4. Which of the following reproductive organs produce sperm cells?
   a. ovaries
   b. vas deferens
   c. fallopian tubes
   d. testes

5. Which of the following reproductive organs produce egg cells?
   a. ovaries
   b. vas deferens
   c. fallopian tubes
   d. testes

Answers

1. a. Budding or fragmentation is the process of producing an outgrowth on some part of the body that can eventually lead a separate life.

2. b. The alternation of generations refers to the formation of two different plant bodies, the sporophyte or the gametophyte, in each generation. This process is most obvious in ferns, but it also happens in flowering plants. The sporophyte generation (usually the most familiar form of the plant) produces spores capable of forming the gametophyte generation (usually a less familiar or more inconspicuous form of the plant). The gametophyte generation then produces the gametes (eggs and sperm), which will join and produce the next sporophyte generation.

3. c. The organs that produce gametes are the ovaries in females and the testes in males. These organs also produce the hormones that cause the development of each gender's physical characteristics.

4. d. Sperm cells are produced by the male in testes.

5. a. Egg cells are produced by the female in ovaries.

In Short

Any living organism has a limited life span, but life itself goes on because organisms can create offspring through reproduction. All the organism Kingdoms have representatives that engage in asexual reproduction, which is an advantage because you do not need to find a partner, and usually, you can reproduce in large numbers very quickly. Sometimes, asexual reproduction is known as vegetative reproduction. Although asexual reproduction allows plants to reproduce quickly and colonize a large area, most plants still engage in sexual reproduction at least part of the time. A plant that sexually reproduces switches between two distinctly different body types, the sporophyte and the gametophyte. Switching from the sporophyte form to the gametophyte form represents the concept of the alternation of generations.

Sexual reproduction in plants or animals depends on the production of two different gametes or sex cells. Male animals produce the smaller, more mobile gamete known as a sperm cell. Females produce the larger, more sedentary gamete known as an egg cell.

19 ▶ Heredity and DNA Science

Organisms exhibit characteristics that define them. For example, an elephant has a trunk, an oak tree has green leaves and makes acorns, and humans have large brains. All these characteristics were inherited from parent organisms that looked and acted similarly. These heritable characteristics are transmitted on structures we call *genes* and *chromosomes*. In sexual reproduction, each parent contributes half of his or her genes to the offspring. The scientific study of heritable traits is called *genetics,* and Gregor Mendel is considered to be the father of genetics from his work with pea plants.

▶ Genes and Chromosomes

Chromosomes are tiny structures within the cell nucleus that are the physical basis of heredity. Certain regions of the chromosomes are designated as genes. Each gene contains the information necessary to produce a single trait in an organism, and each gene is different from any other. For any trait, we inherit one gene from our father and one from our mother. Sometimes, even the genes in these pairs will be slightly different from each other.

Alternate forms of the same gene are called *alleles*. When the alleles are identical, we say that the individual is *homozygous* for that trait (a child may have blue eyes because he or she inherited two identical blue eye color genes from each parent). When the alleles are different, we say the individual is *heterozygous* for that trait (a child may have brown eyes because he or she inherited different eye color genes from each parent).

When genes exist in a heterozygous pairing, usually one is expressed over the other, and we say that it is *dominant*. The unexpressed gene is called *recessive*. With brown versus blue eyes, the allele for brown eyes is dominant over the one for blue eyes. Thus, the heterozygous child with blue and brown genes will have brown eyes. This general principal has many variations and exceptions.

▶ Patterns of Inheritance

Because of the way gametes are formed, we can get some interesting distributions of characteristics in offspring. Biologists refer to the genetic makeup of an organism as its *genotype*. However, the collection of physical characteristics that result from the action of genes is called an organism's *phenotype*. Patterns of inheritance may yield surprising results because the genotype determines the phenotype, but the phenotype may hide some of the unexpressed alleles.

For example, if two blue-eyed parents reproduce, their offspring will have blue eyes because only blue alleles exist within the parents' gametes. However, two brown-eyed parents may actually be able to produce a blue-eyed child. This happens because the blue allele is hidden in the parents. Remember that a brown-eyed person can be that way because both his or her alleles are for brown eyes or because one allele is for brown and the other is for blue. When their gametes form, each parent may produce only gametes with alleles for brown eyes or they might produce gametes that contain the blue allele. If the latter occurs in both parents, then their offspring can have blue eyes even though both have brown eyes.

Molecular Basis of Heredity

Like the rest of the body, heredity is dependent on the functioning of biological molecules. The molecule at the basis of heredity is the long, chain polymer we call *deoxyribonucleic acid* or, more familiarly, DNA. A gene consists of DNA molecules, which are known as polymers. A *polymer* is a very large molecule made up of many similarly repeating units (called *nucleotides* in DNA). The shape of the DNA molecule is a double spiral or *helix*, sort of like a winding staircase with a handrail on each side.

In what is known as the Central Dogma of biology, DNA contains hereditary information, which is transferred (or transcribed) into another molecule called *ribonucleic acid* (RNA), which is then transformed (or translated) into proteins. It is these protein molecules that are responsible for the expression of inherited traits.

Four special molecules called nucleotides are contained within the structure of the larger DNA molecule. These nucleotides are known as *adenine, cytosine, guanine,* and *thymine*. They are commonly abbreviated by their first letters to A, C, G, and T. The arrangement of these nucleotides forms a code that can contain hereditary information. Special enzymes in the cell nucleus read this code and transcribe it into an RNA molecule, specifically known as *messenger RNA,* because it takes the coded message from the nucleus into the cell's cytoplasm. It is here that the small organelles called *ribosomes* translate the coded messenger RNA into protein molecules. These protein molecules are either destined to become structural components (such as in the muscles) or enzymes where they will regulate metabolic reactions. These proteins give us our inherited traits.

Human beings have been manipulating this process for thousands of years. We perform this process when we breed crop animals or plants. In the past, we were clever but not very sophisticated because we had to find the best animal or plant and breed it until we achieved the desired crop. The corn we eat today is very different than the plant called maize from which it was bred. The more sophisticated and technically challenging manipulation of an organism's DNA that we perform today is called *genetic engineering* and is part of the biotechnology industry.

▶ Practice

1. On paired chromosomes, when two alleles are identical, we say the pair is
 a. heterozygous.
 b. homozygous.
 c. a tetrad.
 d. binomial.

2. If a person with a phenotype of brown eyes reproduces with another person who exhibits the brown-eye phenotype, which possibility best describes the type of offspring that could be produced?
 a. only brown-eyed children
 b. only blue-eyed children
 c. neither brown eyed or blue eyed
 d. brown-eyed and blue-eyed children

3. Biology's Central Dogma states that
 a. proteins produce RNA, which is translated into DNA.
 b. DNA is transcribed into RNA, which is translated into proteins.
 c. RNA codes for DNA, which codes for proteins.
 d. DNA is translated into proteins that code for RNA.

4. Which of the following is NOT a nucleotide found in DNA?
 a. uracil
 b. guanine
 c. cytosine
 d. thymine

5. The phenotype describes an organism's
 a. appearance.
 b. genetic code.
 c. type of DNA.
 d. eye color only.

6. The shape of the DNA molecule is a
 a. single spiral.
 b. double spiral.
 c. straight chain.
 d. bent chain.

▶ Answers

1. b. The pair of alleles is called homozygous, and an organism would be homozygous for the trait governed by those alleles.

2. d. Each parent exhibits the brown-eyed pheno-type, so it is possible that only brown-eyed children would be produced. This would be the case if both parents were also homozygous for the brown-eye trait. However, because the brown-eye allele is dominant over the blue-eye allele, you cannot say for certain that the parents are each homozygous for brown eyes or if they are heterozygous. In other words, they may each have one brown-eye allele and one blue-eye allele. If that's the case, then they could end up producing a blue-eyed child if they each contribute a blue-eye gene. So the best answer is that they could produce both brown-eyed and blue-eyed children.

3. b. The Central Dogma of biology states that DNA in the cell's nucleus is transcribed into a messenger RNA molecule, which then leaves the nucleus and enters the cytoplasm. In the cell's cytoplasm, the RNA molecule is trans-lated into a protein molecule.

4. a. Uracil is a nucleotide, but it is found in RNA, not in DNA. The nucleotides in DNA are ane-nine, guanine, cytosine, and thymine.

5. a. The phenotype is the expression of traits as determined by the genotype or genetic infor-mation contained in the organism's DNA.

6. b. DNA is in the shape of a double spiral or dou-ble helix.

▶ In Short

Organisms exhibit characteristics that define them, such as an elephant having a trunk, an oak tree having green leaves, and humans having large brains. All these characteristics were inherited from parent organisms that looked and acted similarly. These heritable char-acteristics are transmitted on structures we call genes and chromosomes. Biologists refer to the genetic makeup of an organism as its genotype. However, the collection of physical characteristics that result from the action of genes is called an organism's phenotype. The molecule at the basis of heredity is the long, chain polymer we call deoxyribonucleic acid or DNA. A gene consists of molecules of DNA. In what is known as the Central Dogma of biology, DNA contains hereditary information, which is transferred (or transcribed) into another molecule called ribonucleic acid (RNA), which is then transformed (or translated) into pro-teins. These protein molecules are responsible for the expression of inherited traits.

20 ▶ Evolution

In general, the term evolution means change over time. In biology, the term *evolution* refers to the transformation of life from its simplest form to the great diversity we see today over billions of years. Animals are constantly responding to their environments and, in that process, may be successful by producing offspring. In this sense, the organisms have evolved to adapt well to their environment. A process of evolution known as *natural selection* is a mechanism of evolution.

▶ Charles Darwin and the Origin of Species

The publication of Charles Darwin's *On the Origin of the Species by Means of Natural Selection* in 1859 gave the world its most clearly stated account of how life developed. His book also addressed the great diversity of living organisms, their interrelationships, their relatedness, and their ability to adapt to various environments. It was a profound, far-reaching theory and forms the basis of modern biology.

Humans have been manipulating other organisms for thousands of years. That's how we ended up with so many dog breeds and most of our crop animals and plants. We notice a trait that we like and want to encourage, and we look for an animal or plant with that characteristic. We then breed that organism with another that has similar traits or other ones we want to encourage. With luck and lots of time, we will eventually end up with an organism that embodies all the traits we want. This is called *artificial selection* because we are specifically picking the desired traits.

In nature, the process of natural selection occurs. In this case, no one picks the desired characteristics. Instead, an organism has characteristics that are either well suited to its environment or it won't have such characteristics. Those with characteristics that fit well with their environment will survive long enough to reproduce and be able to produce resources for their offspring, thus ensuring continuation of their kind. This is where the idea of "survival of the fittest" comes from. Fittest here doesn't necessarily mean the strongest; it means the organism that is best adapted to its environment. Natural selection is the main mechanism of evolution. The theory of natural selection states that diversity has come about by descent from a common ancestor with some modifications. Apes and humans are not the same organism, but we do share a common ancestor we each descended from and we each have been modified through natural selection.

Generally, Darwin's theory contains these facts:

- All species have a great ability to reproduce, and the population of each would increase greatly if all individuals reproduced successfully. The birth of more individuals than the environment can support leads to a struggle among individuals with some surviving. This leads to populations relatively stable in size.
- No two individuals in a population are exactly alike and their variability is inheritable. Therefore, survival depends on inheriting characteristics that best suit the individual to the environment. These individuals will leave more offspring.
- The unequal ability of members of a population to survive and reproduce will cause a change in the makeup of the population, with favorable characteristics accumulating usually over long periods of time. The theory of punctuated equilibrium, which was not proposed by Darwin but is a more modern idea, states that these changes in a population's makeup can occur relatively quickly.

- Evolution is not guided; it does not aim toward a final, finished product. It modifies populations over time and will continue to do so, even for our species. All life forms share in this gradual change and have shared in it over vast periods of time so that in a sense, bacteria are as highly evolved in their own very different ways as human beings.

▶ The Special Case of Human Beings

We humans are less influenced by our environment because we can use technology to protect ourselves. In this way, evolutionary changes in our population may be delayed. A good example of this phenomenon is seen by looking at common eyeglasses and contact lenses. Under the influence of natural selection, humans with bad eyesight would not survive very long and may not reproduce. Thus, only those with good eyesight would produce offspring. Over a relatively short time span, we would thus end up with most humans having good eyesight. That is not the case because we help those with poor eyesight survive by exercising our technological talents and producing eyeglasses and contact lenses. This shows our compassion, but it removes us from evolutionary pressures.

Unfortunately, our unique ability to control our environment to a very high degree and thus those factors that might limit our population growth leads to unrestrained growth, and our population has been increasing rapidly for centuries. It could be that human population growth is the greatest environmental threat as we crowd out other species, destroy habitats, use up resources, and pollute with our wastes. It is in the interest of all life on Earth that we use our highly evolved brains to find solutions to population growth and its ill effects without losing our compassion.

▶ **Practice**

1. The mechanism behind evolution is known as
   a. artificial selection.
   b. mate selection.
   c. natural selection.
   d. punctuated selection.

2. Which of the following is NOT a basic assumption of Darwin's theory of evolution?
   a. All species have a great ability to reproduce, and the population of each would increase greatly if all individuals reproduced successfully.
   b. No two individuals in a population are exactly alike and their variability is inheritable.
   c. Survival depends on inheriting characteristics that best suit the individual to the environment.
   d. All individuals in a population will survive and be able to reproduce.

3. Poor eyesight in humans is an example of
   a. how well adapted to the environment humans are.
   b. a trait that is favorable in most environments.
   c. a trait that will allow for greater reproductive success.
   d. a trait that we are artificially selecting for in our populations.

4. The many breeds of dogs we see today are the result of which of these processes?
   a. translation
   b. artificial selection
   c. natural selection
   d. punctuated selection

5. Which of the following statements is NOT true about Charles Darwin's theory of evolution?
   a. Organisms evolve through a mechanism of natural selection.
   b. Each organism in a population is exactly like every other organism in that population.
   c. Organisms have a great ability to reproduce.
   d. Evolution modifies organisms over time.

▶ Answers

1. c. Natural selection occurs when animals well adapted to their environment are able to reproduce and leave more offspring than those animals who are not well adapted. This advantage leads to certain organisms prospering while others fail to survive. Over time, this will preserve and even enhance characteristics in the surviving population.

2. d. Only the organisms best suited to their environment and able to obtain resources will be likely to reproduce and leave more offspring.

3. d. People with poor eyesight would most likely not be able to survive if it weren't for the fact that our society supports them; therefore, we are artificially selecting for that trait. Natural selection would lead to a population with very good eyesight if it weren't for our intervention. This can be a good and compassionate behavior for a society to engage in; however, rampant human population growth without paying attention to natural controls will leave the Earth a poorer quality place for all organisms.

4. b. Artificial selection by humans has resulted in many types of dogs bred specifically for some purpose of our own.

5. b. It is not true that every organism in a population is just exactly like all others; in fact, the opposite is true. These differences are inheritable and can be acted upon by natural selection.

▶ In Short

In general, the term evolution means change over time. In biology, the term evolution refers to the transformation of life from its simplest form to the great diversity we see today over billions of years. Humans have been manipulating other organisms for thousands of years. This is called artificial selection because we are specifically picking the desired traits.

In nature, the process of natural selection occurs. In this case, no one chooses the desired characteristics. Instead, an organism will have characteristics that are either well suited to their environment or they won't have such characteristics. Those with characteristics that fit well with their environment will survive long enough to reproduce and be able to produce resources for their offspring, thus ensuring continuation of their kind. It is in the interest of all life on Earth that we use our highly evolved brains to find solutions to population growth and its ill effects without losing our compassion.

Posttest

If you have completed all 20 lessons in this book, then you are ready to take the posttest to measure your progress. The posttest has 35 multiple-choice questions covering the topics you studied in this book. Although the format of the posttest is similar to that of the pretest, the questions are different.

Take as much time as you need to complete the posttest. When you are finished, check your answers with the answer key at the end of the chapter. Along with each answer is the lesson that covers the particular topic. Once you know your score on the posttest, compare the results with the pretest. If you scored better on the posttest than you did on the pretest, look at the questions you missed, if any. Do you know why you missed the question, or do you need to go back to the lesson and review the concept?

If your score on the posttest doesn't show much improvement, take a second look at the questions you missed. Did you miss a question because of an error you made? If you can figure out why you missed the question, then you understand the concept and just need to concentrate more on accuracy when taking a test. If you missed a question because you did not understand the information, go back to the lesson and spend more time reading over the concept. Take the time to understand basic biology thoroughly. You need a solid foundation in basic biology if you plan to use this information or progress to a higher level. Whatever your score on this posttest, keep this book for review and future reference. Use the following grid to record your answers.

1.	ⓐ ⓑ ⓒ ⓓ	13.	ⓐ ⓑ ⓒ ⓓ	25.	ⓐ ⓑ ⓒ ⓓ
2.	ⓐ ⓑ ⓒ ⓓ	14.	ⓐ ⓑ ⓒ ⓓ	26.	ⓐ ⓑ ⓒ ⓓ
3.	ⓐ ⓑ ⓒ ⓓ	15.	ⓐ ⓑ ⓒ ⓓ	27.	ⓐ ⓑ ⓒ ⓓ
4.	ⓐ ⓑ ⓒ ⓓ	16.	ⓐ ⓑ ⓒ ⓓ	28.	ⓐ ⓑ ⓒ ⓓ
5.	ⓐ ⓑ ⓒ ⓓ	17.	ⓐ ⓑ ⓒ ⓓ	29.	ⓐ ⓑ ⓒ ⓓ
6.	ⓐ ⓑ ⓒ ⓓ	18.	ⓐ ⓑ ⓒ ⓓ	30.	ⓐ ⓑ ⓒ ⓓ
7.	ⓐ ⓑ ⓒ ⓓ	19.	ⓐ ⓑ ⓒ ⓓ	31.	ⓐ ⓑ ⓒ ⓓ
8.	ⓐ ⓑ ⓒ ⓓ	20.	ⓐ ⓑ ⓒ ⓓ	32.	ⓐ ⓑ ⓒ ⓓ
9.	ⓐ ⓑ ⓒ ⓓ	21.	ⓐ ⓑ ⓒ ⓓ	33.	ⓐ ⓑ ⓒ ⓓ
10.	ⓐ ⓑ ⓒ ⓓ	22.	ⓐ ⓑ ⓒ ⓓ	34.	ⓐ ⓑ ⓒ ⓓ
11.	ⓐ ⓑ ⓒ ⓓ	23.	ⓐ ⓑ ⓒ ⓓ	35.	ⓐ ⓑ ⓒ ⓓ
12.	ⓐ ⓑ ⓒ ⓓ	24.	ⓐ ⓑ ⓒ ⓓ		

1. Blood moving through the pulmonary vein is
   a. oxygenated.
   b. not oxygenated.
   c. mixed oxygenated and nonoxygenated blood.
   d. full of carbon dioxide.

2. How are sponges and coelenterates different?
   a. Coelenterates have nerve cells; sponges do not.
   b. Coelenterates have bony skeletons; sponges do not.
   c. Sponges are marine animals; coelenterates are not.
   d. Sponges are multicellular; coelenterates are not.

3. The left ventricle of the heart contains which of the following?
   a. nonoxygenated blood
   b. oxygenated blood
   c. mixed oxygenated and nonoxygenated blood
   d. blood with lots of carbon dioxide

4. Which of the following is the site of protein synthesis within a eukaryotic cell?
   a. the ribosomes
   b. the nucleus
   c. the mitochondria
   d. the Golgi apparatus

5. On some invertebrates, what is the hard outer coating called?
   a. the cilia
   b. the whiskers
   c. the epidermis
   d. the exoskeleton

6. What are the tiny air sacs where the exchange of respiratory gases occurs in vertebrates?
   a. the bronchioles
   b. the bronchi
   c. the sinuses
   d. the alveoli

7. Which of the following is considered an accessory organ in the digestive system?
   a. the mouth
   b. the esophagus
   c. the liver
   d. the pharynx

8. What is the fluid portion of our blood called?
   a. protoplasm
   b. plasma
   c. adrenaline
   d. urine

9. The process by which a population of organisms adapts to their environment over time is called
   a. evolution.
   b. reproduction.
   c. mutation.
   d. acclimatization.

10. What are the two kinds of chambers of the heart, and how are they different from one another?

   a. A superior vena cava pumps blood to areas above the heart, and an inferior vena cava pumps blood to the lower body.

   b. A superior vena cava pumps blood to the lower body, and an inferior vena cava pumps blood to areas above the heart.

   c. An atrium pumps blood away from the heart, and a ventricle receives blood coming from the body.

   d. An atrium receives blood coming into the heart from the body, and a ventricle pumps blood away from the heart.

11. In order to be considered organic, a compound must contain which of the following elements?

   a. hydrogen

   b. sodium

   c. nitrogen

   d. carbon

12. Which of the following is an organelle?

   a. heart

   b. chloroplast

   c. liver

   d. fibrin

13. Which of the following is a vertebrate?

   a. sponge

   b. sea star

   c. octopus

   d. snake

14. Which of the following plants lacks a vascular system?

   a. moss

   b. fern

   c. fir tree

   d. peanut plant

15. Which of the following is an abiotic factor in the life of a zebra?

   a. grasses

   b. trees

   c. water

   d. lions

16. When a plant is placed near a sunny window, the plant's stem grows toward the light. This is an example of

   a. phototropism.

   b. gravitropism.

   c. germination.

   d. transpiration.

17. Complete the two missing parts of the following food chain: X $\rightarrow$ plant $\rightarrow$ X $\rightarrow$ snake

   a. water, owl

   b. water, mouse

   c. sunlight, deer

   d. sunlight, mouse

18. In a food chain, which of the following are the producers?

   a. dead organic matter

   b. plant-eating animals

   c. meat-eating animals

   d. green plants

19. Which of the following best describes what an herbivore eats?

   a. animal matter only

   b. plant matter only

   c. detritus only

   d. both animal and plant matter

20. A neuron is a

   a. muscle cell.

   b. kidney cell.

   c. bone cell.

   d. nerve cell.

21. Which of the following normal body fluids is a suspension?

   a. blood

   b. perspiration

   c. saliva

   d. tears

22. In the scientific name for the emperor penguin, *Aptenodytes forsteri*, the word *Aptenodytes* indicates the

   a. phylum.

   b. order.

   c. species.

   d. genus.

23. Messenger RNA is used as a template to produce which of the following?

   a. lipids

   b. proteins

   c. carbohydrates

   d. hydrocarbons

24. What are the blood vessels that carry blood toward the heart?

   a. arteries

   b. veins

   c. capillaries

   d. arterioles

25. Which of the following is the region between two nerve cells across which electronic impulses are transmitted?

   a. neuron

   b. myelin sheath

   c. synapse

   d. axon

26. Which of the following actions is controlled by smooth muscles?

   a. running

   b. heartbeat

   c. peristalsis

   d. movement of bones and joints

27. Which of the following groups of organisms produce flowers?

   a. angiosperms

   b. gymnosperms

   c. mosses

   d. fungi

28. Atoms are arranged according to the number of

   a. electrons in the nucleus.

   b. electrons around the nucleus.

   c. protons in the nucleus.

   d. protons around the nucleus.

29. Nucleic acids are large molecules made up of smaller molecules called
   a. amino acids.
   b. nucleotides.
   c. lipids.
   d. carbohydrates.

30. Which of the following is true of nonliving matter?
   a. It reacts to environmental stimuli.
   b. It is able to reproduce itself.
   c. It undergoes chemical breakdown.
   d. It has a high level of complexity.

31. Irritability refers to an organism's ability to
   a. reproduce.
   b. respond to environmental stimuli.
   c. adapt to its environment.
   d. grow and develop.

32. Bacteria are part of which of the following Kingdoms?
   a. Protist
   b. Monera
   c. Animal
   d. Plant

33. Which of the following organisms form hyphae and mycelium tissue?
   a. oak tree
   b. whale
   c. amoeba
   d. mushroom

34. The system of classifying organisms developed by Carlos Linneaus is called
   a. bipartional nomenclature.
   b. binomial nomenclature.
   c. fission nomenclature.
   d. binary nomenclature.

35. Which of the following plant groups produces seeds in cones?
   a. angiosperms
   b. bryophytes
   c. all vascular plants
   d. gymnosperms

▶ Answers

If you miss any of the answers, you can find help in the lesson shown to the right of the correct answer.

1. a.	Lesson 15	**20.** d. Lesson 17
2. d.	Lesson 6	**21.** a. Lesson 15
3. b.	Lesson 15	**22.** d. Lesson 3
4. a.	Lesson 10	**23.** b. Lesson 19
5. d.	Lesson 12	**24.** b. Lesson 15
6. d.	Lesson 14	**25.** c. Lesson 17
7. c.	Lesson 11	**26.** c. Lesson 11
8. b.	Lesson 15	**27.** a. Lesson 5
9. a.	Lesson 20	**28.** c. Lesson 1
10. d.	Lesson 15	**29.** b. Lesson 1
11. d.	Lesson 1	**30.** c. Lesson 2
12. b.	Lesson 3	**31.** b. Lesson 17
13. d.	Lesson 6	**32.** b. Lesson 3
14. a.	Lesson 5	**33.** d. Lesson 4
15. c.	Lesson 7	**34.** b. Lesson 3
16. a.	Lesson 17	**35.** d. Lesson 5
17. d.	Lesson 7	
18. d.	Lesson 7	
19. b.	Lesson 7	

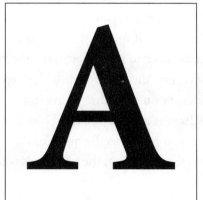

How to Prepare for a Test

A standardized test is nothing to fear. Many people worry about a testing situation, but you're much better off taking that nervous energy and turning it into something positive that will help you do well on your test, rather than inhibit your testing ability. The following pages include valuable tips for combating test anxiety, that sinking or blank feeling some people get as they begin a test or encounter a difficult question. You will also find valuable tips for using your time wisely and for avoiding errors in a testing situation. Finally, you will find a plan for preparing for the test, a plan for the test day, and a suggestion for a posttest activity.

▶ Combating Test Anxiety

Knowing what to expect and being prepared are the best defense against test anxiety, that worrisome feeling that keeps you from doing your best. Practice and preparation keeps you from succumbing to that anxiety. Nevertheless, even the brightest, most well-prepared test takers may suffer from occasional bouts of test anxiety. But don't worry; you can overcome it.

Take the Test One Question at a Time
Focus all your attention on the one question you're answering. Block out any thoughts about questions you've already read or concerns about what's coming next. Concentrate your thinking where it will do the most good—on the question you're answering.

Develop a Positive Attitude

Keep reminding yourself that you're prepared. The fact that you have read this book means that you're better prepared than most taking the test. Remember, it's only a test, and you're going to do your best. That's all anyone can ask of you. If that nagging drill sergeant voice inside your head starts sending negative messages, combat them with positive ones of your own:

- "I'm doing just fine."
- "I've prepared for this test."
- "I know exactly what to do."
- "I know I can get the score I'm shooting for."

You get the idea. Remember to drown out negative messages with positive ones of your own.

If You Lose Your Concentration

Don't worry about it! It's normal. During a long test, it happens to everyone. When your mind is stressed or overexerted, it takes a break whether you want it to or not. It's easy to get your concentration back if you simply acknowledge the fact that you've lost it and take a quick break. You brain needs very little time (seconds really) to rest.

Put your pencil down and close your eyes. Take a few deep breaths and listen to the sound of your breathing. The ten seconds or so that this takes is really all the time your brain needs to relax and get ready to focus again.

Try this technique several times in the days before the test when you feel stressed. The more you practice, the better it will work for you on the day of the test.

If You Freeze before or during the Test

Don't worry about a question that stumps you, even though you're sure you know the answer. Mark it and go on to the next question. You can come back to the "stumper" later. Try to put it out of your mind completely until you come back to it. Just let your subconscious mind chew on the question while your conscious mind focuses on the other items (one at a time, of course). Chances are, the memory block will be gone by the time you return to the question.

If you freeze before you begin the test, here's what to do:

1. Take a little time to look over the test.
2. Read a few of the questions.
3. Decide which ones are the easiest and start there.
4. Before long, you'll be "in the groove."

▶ Time Strategies

Use your time wisely to avoid making careless errors.

Pace Yourself

The most important time strategy is pacing yourself. Before you begin, take just a few seconds to survey the test, making note of the number of questions and of the sections that look easier than the rest. Plan a rough time schedule based on the amount of time available to you. Mark the halfway point on your test and indicate what the time will be when the testing period is half over.

Keep Moving

Once you begin the test, keep moving. If you work slowly in an attempt to make fewer mistakes, your mind will become bored and begin to wander. You'll end up making far more mistakes if you're not concentrating.

As long as we're talking about mistakes, don't stop for difficult questions. Skip them and move on. You can come back to them later if you have time. A question that takes you five seconds to answer counts as much as one that takes you several minutes, so pick up the easy points first. Besides, answering the easier questions first helps build your confidence and gets you in the testing groove. Who knows? As you go through the test, you may even stumble across some relevant information to help you answer those tough questions.

Don't Rush

Keep moving, but don't rush. Think of your mind as a seesaw. On one side is your emotional energy; on the other side is your intellectual energy. When your emotional energy is high, your intellectual capacity is low. Remember how difficult it is to reason with someone when you're angry? On the other hand, when your intellectual energy is high, your emotional energy is low. Rushing raises your emotional energy. Remember the last time you were late for work? All that rushing around causes you to forget important things, such as your lunch. Move quickly to keep your mind from wandering, but don't rush and get yourself flustered.

Check Yourself

Check yourself at the halfway mark. If you're a little ahead, you know you're on track and may even have a little time left to check your work. If you're a little behind, you have several choices. You can pick up the pace a little, but do this only if you can do it comfortably. Remember—don't rush! You can also skip around in the remaining portion of the test to pick up as many easy points as possible. This strategy has one drawback, however. If you are marking a bubble-style answer sheet, and you put the right answers in the wrong bubbles, they're wrong. So pay close attention to the question numbers if you decide to do this.

▶ Avoiding Errors

When you take the test, you want to make as few errors as possible in the questions you answer. Here are a few tactics to keep in mind.

Control Yourself

Remember the comparison between your mind and a seesaw that you read about a few paragraphs ago? Keeping your emotional energy low and your intellectual energy high is the best way to avoid mistakes. If you feel stressed or worried, stop for a few seconds. Acknowledge the feeling (Hmmm! I'm feeling a little pressure here!), take a few deep breaths, and send yourself a few positive messages. This relieves your emotional anxiety and boosts your intellectual capacity.

Directions

In many standardized testing situations, a proctor reads the instructions aloud. Make certain you understand what is expected. If you don't, ask. Listen carefully for instructions about how to answer the questions and make certain you know how much time you have to complete the task. Write the time on your test if you don't already know how long you have. If you miss this vital information, ask for it. You need it to do well.

Answers

Place your answers in the right blanks or in the corresponding ovals on the answer sheet. Right answers in the wrong place earn no points. It's a good idea to check every five to ten questions to make sure you're in the right spot. That way you won't need much time to correct your answer sheet if you have made an error.

▶ Reading Long Passages

Frequently, standardized tests are designed to test your reading comprehension. The reading sections often contain passages that are a paragraph or more. Here are a few tactics for approaching these sections.

This may seem strange, but some questions can be answered without ever reading the passage. If the passage is short, a paragraph around four sentences or so, read the questions first. You may be able to answer them by using your common sense. You can check your answers later after you've actually read the passage. Even if you can't answer any of the questions, you know what to look for in the passage. This focuses your reading and makes it easier for you to retain important information. Most questions will deal with isolated details in the passage. If you know what to look for ahead of time, it's easier to find the information.

If a reading passage is long and followed by more than ten questions, you may end up spending too much time reading the questions first. Even so, take a few seconds to skim the questions and read a few of the shorter ones. As you read, mark up the passage. If you find a sentence that seems to state the main idea of the passage, underline it. As you read through the rest of the passage, number the main points that support the main idea. Several questions will deal with this information, and if it's underlined and numbered, you can locate it easily. Other questions will ask for specific details. Circle information that tells who, what, when, or where. The circles will be easy to locate later if you run across a question that asks for specific information. Marking up a passage this way also heightens your concentration and makes it more likely that you'll remember the information when you answer the questions following the passage.

Choosing the Right Answers

Make sure you understand what the question is asking. If you're not sure of what's being asked, you'll never know whether you've chosen the right answer, so figure out what the question is asking. If the answer isn't readily apparent, look for clues in the answer choices. Notice the similarities and differences. Sometimes, this helps put the question in a new perspective and makes it easier to answer. If you're still not sure of the answer, use the process of elimination. First, eliminate any answer choices that are obviously wrong. Then reason your way through the remaining choices. You may be able to use relevant information from other parts of the test. If you can't eliminate any of the answer choices, you might be better off to skip the question and come back to it later. If you can't eliminate any answer choices to improve your odds when you come back later, then make a guess and move on.

If You're Penalized for Wrong Answers

You must know, before you begin the test, whether wrong answers are penalized. If you don't, ask the proctor before the test begins. Whether you make a guess depends on the penalty. Some standardized tests are scored in such a way that every wrong answer reduces your score by one-fourth or one-half a point. Whatever the penalty, if you can eliminate enough choices to make the odds of answering the question better than the penalty for getting it wrong, make a guess.

Let's imagine you are taking a test in which each answer has four choices and you are penalized one-fourth a point for each wrong answer. If you have no clue and cannot eliminate any of the answer choices, you're better off leaving the question blank because the odds of answering correctly are one in four. This makes the penalty and the odds equal. However, if you can eliminate one of the choices, the odds are now in your favor. You have a one in three chance of answering the question correctly. Fortunately, few tests are scored using such elaborate means, but if your test is one of them, know the penalties and calculate your odds before you take a guess on a question.

If You Finish Early

Use any time you have left at the end of the test or test section to check your work. First, make certain you've put the answers in the right places. As you're doing this, make sure you've answered each question only once. Most standardized tests are scored in such a way that questions with more than one answer are marked wrong. If you've erased an answer, make sure you've done a good job. Also, check for stray marks on your answer sheet that could distort your score.

After you've checked for these obvious errors, take a second look at the more difficult questions. You've probably heard the folk wisdom about never changing an answer. If you have a good reason for thinking a response is wrong, change it.

▶ The Days before the Test

To get ready for a challenge like a big exam, you have to take control of your physical state as well as your mental state. Exercise, proper diet, and rest will ensure that your body works with—rather than against—your mind on test day, as well as during your preparation.

Physical Activity

Get some exercise in the days preceding the test. You'll send some extra oxygen to your brain and allow your thinking performance to peak on the day you take the test. Moderation is the key here. You don't want to exercise so much that you feel exhausted, but a little physical activity will invigorate your body and brain.

Balanced Diet

Like your body, your brain needs the proper nutrients to function well. Eat plenty of fruits and vegetables in the days before the test. Foods that are high in lecithin, such as fish and beans, are especially good choices. Lecithin is a mineral your brain needs for peak performance. You may even consider a visit to your local pharmacy to buy a bottle of lecithin tablets several weeks before your test.

Rest

Get plenty of sleep the nights before you take the test. Don't overdo it, though, or you'll make yourself as groggy as if you were overtired. Go to bed at a reasonable time, early enough to get the number of hours you need to function effectively. You'll feel relaxed and rested if you've gotten plenty of sleep in the days before you take the test.

Trial Run

At some point before you take the test, make a trial run to the testing center to see how long it takes. Rushing raises your emotional energy and lowers your intellectual capacity, so you want to allow plenty of time on test day to get to the testing center. Arriving ten or fifteen minutes early gives you time to relax and get situated.

Test Day

It's finally here, the day of the big test. Set your alarm early enough to allow plenty of time. Eat a good breakfast and avoid anything that's really high in sugar, such as donuts. A sugar high turns into a sugar low after an hour or so. Cereal and toast or anything with complex carbohydrates is a good choice. Eat only moderate amounts. You don't want to take a test feeling stuffed!

Pack a high-energy snack to take with you because you may have a break sometime during the test when you can grab a quick snack. Bananas are great. They have a moderate amount of sugar and plenty of brain nutrients such as potassium. Most proctors won't allow you to eat a snack while you're testing, but a peppermint shouldn't pose a problem. Peppermints are like smelling salts for your brain. If you lose your concentration or suffer from a momentary mental block, a peppermint can get you back on track. Don't forget the earlier advice about relaxing and taking a few deep breaths.

Leave early enough so you have plenty of time to get to the test center. Allow a few minutes for unexpected traffic. When you arrive, locate the restroom and use it. Few things interfere with concentration as much as a full bladder. Then find your seat and make sure it's comfortable. If it isn't, tell the proctor and ask to move to a more suitable seat.

Now relax and think positively! Before you know it, the test will be over, and you'll walk away knowing you've done as well as you can.

After the Test

Do two things:

1. Plan a little celebration.
2. Go to it.

If you have something to look forward to after the test is over, you may find it easier to prepare well for the exam and keep moving during the test. Good luck!

Glossary

abiotic   refers to nonliving things; the important abiotic factors of the environment include light, temperature, moisture, and atmospheric gases.

aerobic   refers to the presence of the gas oxygen; aerobic respiration is a cellular metabolic function that uses oxygen.

allele   one member of a pair of genes that occupy a specific position on a specific chromosome.

alveolus   a tiny, thin-walled sac in the lungs that is rich in capillaries and acts as the exchange site for oxygen and carbon dioxide; the plural is alveoli.

actin   a protein in muscle that acts in conjunction with myosin during muscle contraction.

arteriole   the small terminal branch of an artery that connects to a capillary.

aorta   the main artery that carries blood away from the left ventricle of the heart to the rest of the body (except for the lungs).

anabolism   the phase of metabolism in which simple substances are built up into the complex materials of living tissue (see also catabolism, the opposite process).

anaerobic   biochemical processes that proceed in the absence of oxygen; the yeast fermentation of sugar to beer or wine is anaerobic respiration.

antagonistic pairs muscles are arranged in pairs; when one contracts, the other relaxes, and a limb will move toward the contracting muscle. To move the limb back to its original starting position, the relaxed muscle will have to contract and the contracted muscle will have to relax. In this sense, the muscles are working in opposition to each other (they are "antagonistic" toward each other).

amino acid the organic molecules that, when linked together by chemical bonds, form proteins.

amphibian a cold-blooded, smooth-skinned vertebrate; examples are frogs and salamanders. Usually, they hatch from eggs and start life breathing with gills. They then grow through a metamorphosis that changes them into air-breathing adults.

angiosperm the name we give to seed plants that form flowers. These plants now dominate the earth (even more so than the gymnosperms) and are highly diverse with many different types of plants. The angiosperms have been so successful because they developed flowers, fruits, and broad leaves.

Animal Kingdom the organisms classified into this Kingdom are multicellular and, because they do not have chlorophyll, are unable to produce their own food. Herbivore animals eat plants, carnivore animals eat meat (other animals), and omnivores eat both plants and animals.

animate refers to a living being.

artificial selection the process in which humans choose desirable traits in animals or plants and breed the organisms that exhibit only those traits. This results in a new species with characteristics that we find desirable but that may not necessarily be best adapted to a natural environment. This has been used for thousands of years to produce crop animals and plants; this contrasts with natural selection.

asexual reproduction reproduction that does not involve the union of sperm and egg. It is accomplished in processes such as budding, fragmentation, and binary fission (splitting into two); many animals and plants have asexual reproduction as part of their life cycle.

alternation of generations the regular alternation of forms of reproduction in the life cycle of organisms.

atoms a unit of matter; it is the smallest unit of an element and consists of protons, neutrons, and electrons. A single atom of an element will have the properties of that element and thus is the smallest piece of that element; however, the atom itself consists of even smaller particles that do not have the properties of that particular element because they are the same in every atom of every element.

autonomic nervous system part of the peripheral nervous system that is not under conscious control. It is responsible for critical life functions such as breathing and heart rate. It also has two divisions, the sympathetic nervous system and the parasympathetic nervous system.

autotroph an organism capable of producing its own food from inorganic substances such as carbon dioxide and water using light. Green plants and algae, as well as some bacteria and protists, are autotrophs.

axon a long extension of a neuron (nerve cell) that usually conducts impulses away from the cell body; it releases neurotransmitters at its end that cross the gap (synapse) to the next neuron in line.

bacteria microorganisms that do not have a true nucleus; their genetic material is free floating within the cell. Bacteria are very small one-celled organisms, and they do not contain very complex cell structures. Bacteria generally come in three varieties: bacilli (rod-shaped), cocci (sphere-shaped), and spirilla (spiral-shaped). Bacteria are prevalent in all environments and are important members of an ecosystem.

binary fission a method of asexual reproduction that involves splitting a parent cell into two separate cells; used extensively by bacteria.

binomial nomenclature the classification system developed by Carlos Linneaus. It is called binomial nomenclature because any organism can be positively identified by two Latin words, the Genus and species words, that specifically name an organism. The Genus name is always capitalized and written in italics, whereas the species name is written lowercase but also in italics. The European wolf is *Canis lupus, Canis familiaris* is the common dog, *Felis tigrina* is a tiger, *Felis domesticus* is a common cat, and humans are *Homo sapiens.*

biome a major regional community of living organisms, such as a grassland or desert that can be described by the dominant forms of plant life and the climate of the area.

biosphere the part of the Earth and its atmosphere where living organisms exist; the area of the Earth's surface and atmosphere that is capable of supporting life.

biotic refers to life or living organisms.

birds a vertebrate organism that is warm blooded, egg laying, and feathered; the front limbs are wings, and they are usually able to fly.

blood a specialized fluid in the circulatory system that consists of red and white blood cells, plasma, and platelets. Blood is the vital fluid that carries oxygen and food molecules to the cells, and carbon dioxide and wastes away from the cells. It also transports the immune system cells that fight infections and disease.

brain a highly specialized organ where neurons have been grouped together into many specific areas, each with a particular function. The brain integrates all the signals in the nervous system and controls the body. It acts as a data storage organ by learning and keeping memories, and is the seat of the conscious mind in higher mammals and other vertebrate animals.

bronchioles a fine, small branching of a bronchus; bronchioles lead directly to alveoli.

bronchus one of two main branches of the trachea that leads into the lungs; its plural is bronchi.

bryophyte (nonvascular plant) these plants lack roots, leaves, and stems, but they do have structures called rhizoids (root-like hairs) that absorb water and nutrients.

budding a process of asexual reproduction in which an offshoot of an organism's body develops into a complete individual; it is used extensively in fungi and animals such as coral.

capillary a tiny blood vessel that connects arterioles and venules; they form an intricate network or web that allows for the exchange of oxygen and carbon dioxide between the blood and body cells.

carbohydrate a group of organic molecules that includes sugars, starch, and cellulose, which are a major source of energy in an animal's diet and in the metabolism of plants. These substances also form the main support structure of plants; carbohydrates are produced by plants during photosynthesis.

carbon dioxide an odorless, colorless gas (abbreviated as CO_2), it is used by plants in photosynthesis to produce organic compounds; it is produced by animals (and plants) as they respire and metabolize organic molecules.

cardiac muscle type of muscle tissue found only in the heart; this type of muscle tissue is so specialized to contract that it will continue to do so even without stimulation from the nervous system, although the contraction will not be coordinated or regular.

carnivore (secondary consumer) animals that eat other animals; because they eat herbivores, carnivores occupy the third trophic level of a food chain and are also known as secondary consumers (the first trophic level is occupied by plants as producers and the second is occupied by herbivores as primary consumers). Animals that consume other carnivores can be considered tertiary consumers.

cartilage connective tissue found in various parts of the body (joints, outer ear, nose) and is a major constituent of young vertebrate skeletons; it is converted to bone as the organism grows and develops.

catabolism the phase of metabolism in which complex molecules are broken down into simpler ones, usually resulting in the release of energy (also see anabolism, the opposite process).

cell the smallest unit of an organism that is capable of independent functioning; it usually has a nucleus, cytoplasm, and various organelles, all surrounded by a cell membrane

cell membrane the membrane that encloses the cytoplasm of a cell.

cell wall the rigid, outermost cell layer found in plants and bacteria; it is not present in animal cells and adds support to the plant.

central dogma the theory in biology that states that DNA contains hereditary information that is transcribed into RNA molecules, which are then translated into protein molecules, which then produce a physical trait in an organism. The process proceeds in that direction only, not in reverse.

central nervous system consists of the brain and spinal cord; it controls the functions of the body in both a conscious as well as an unconscious manner.

chlorophyll a green pigment found in the chloroplasts of plants and other photosynthetic organisms; it is used to absorb sunlight energy, which is then used to fuel the photosynthesis process.

chloroplast a small cellular organelle that contains chlorophyll and is found in photosynthetic organisms such as plants, algae, and some protists.

chromosome a linear strand of DNA and proteins in cells that carries the genes and functions in the transmission of hereditary information.

chyme a thick, soft mass of partly digested food that is produced in the stomach and passed into the small intestines to be acted upon by digestive enzymes.

cilia the very tiny, hair-like projections extending from the surface of a cell; they aid in the movement of the cell itself or in the movement of any fluid around itself.

circulatory system the organ system consisting of the heart, blood vessels, and blood; it acts to pump blood around the body and thus transport oxygen and food molecules to the cells, and carbon dioxide and wastes away from the cells.

classification scheme a system used to organize the living organisms on Earth that includes the following groupings:

Kingdom Animal

Phylum Chordates (this means the wolf had a notochord that developed into its backbone)

Class Mammals (this means the wolf has hair, it bears live young, and nurses them with mammary glands)

Order Carnivores (this means the wolf is a meat eater)

Family Canids (this means the wolf has non-retractable claws, a long muzzle, and separate toes)

Genus *Canis* (this means the wolf is a member of the dog family)

Species *lupus* (this refers to a particular type of wolf known as the European wolf)

covalent bond a chemical bond formed by the sharing of one or more electrons between atoms.

dendrite multiple extensions at one end of a nerve cell (neuron) that receive a neurotransmitter signal from a preceding neuron and transmit an electrical impulse inward toward the cell body; a single neuron may possess many dendrites.

deoxyribonucleic acid (DNA) a molecule belonging to the nucleic acids group that carries the genetic information and is located in the cell's nucleus. DNA consists of two long chains of nucleotides twisted into a double spiral (a helix); four distinct base molecules are used to make the nucleotides in DNA: adenine, guanine, cytosine, and thymine. The sequence of nucleotides determines the protein molecule that will be produced and thus the trait that will be exhibited.

detritivore small, mostly invertebrate animals such as pillbugs, dung beetles, and worms that eat decaying organic matter such as dried leaves. The dead organic matter is known as detritus (litter) and the organisms are called detritivores (detritus or litter eaters). They perform a valuable service in the ecosystem as they break down large pieces of organic matter into pieces small enough for bacteria and funguses to decompose completely.

DNA an abbreviation for deoxyribonucleic acid.

dominant designates a gene (allele) that produces a physical effect (an effect that appears as part of the phenotype) when present with a recessive gene (allele) or when present with a similar dominant allele for the same trait. It is expressed as part of the phenotype when it is present in the homozygous state (two copies of the dominant allele are present) and when in the heterozygous state (where it is present with a recessive allele).

ecology the science that studies the relationships between organisms and their physical environment.

ecosystem a combination of biotic and abiotic components through which energy flows and inorganic material recycles; an ecological community together with its physical environment that functions as a whole unit.

egg cell the female gamete.

electron a negatively charged subatomic particle found in layers surrounding the nucleus of an atom; it has very little mass. Interaction between electrons is the basis of chemical reactions and chemical bond formation.

element a substance composed of identical atoms; using ordinary chemical means, elements cannot be reduced to simpler substances without losing their unique properties.

endoskeleton an internal supporting skeleton composed of bones; it is found in vertebrates and is often just called the skeleton.

enzymes a protein molecule that acts as a catalyst in biochemical reactions; enzymes speed up the rate of a biochemical reaction.

evolution a change, over time, in the genetic composition of a population during many generations as a result of natural selection acting upon the genetic variation inherent among individual organisms in the population. It results in the development of a new species.

exoskeleton a hard outer structure that provides protection or support for some invertebrate organisms such as insects and crustaceans (lobsters and crabs).

fish a cold-blooded vertebrate living in an aquatic environment; it has fins, gills, and a streamlined body for swimming.

flagellum a long, thread-like projection used by some single cells or some single-celled organisms to move with a whip-like motion.

food chain a chain of organisms in an ecological community through which food energy passes from one organism to another as each consumes a lower member and, in turn, is preyed upon by an organism at a higher trophic level.

food web a web of interconnected food chains in an ecological community.

fragmentation a process of asexual reproduction in which a portion of a whole organism can grow into a whole organism; this is used extensively in multicellular invertebrates such as sea stars.

Fungi Kingdom organisms in this Kingdom have some characteristics of plants and other characteristics that make them more animal-like. They lack chlorophyll and cannot perform photosynthesis, so they don't produce their own food and are called heterotrophs. However, they reproduce by spores like plants do.

gamete the sex cells produced by either male or female that join together during sexual reproduction; sperm in males, egg cells in females.

gametophyte the gamete-producing phase of a plant during alternation of generations.

gastrula in animals, this is a stage of the embryo following the blastula and consists of a hollow ball of cells.

gene a sequence of DNA that occupies a specific location on a chromosome and determines a particular characteristic of an organism.

genotype the genetic makeup of an organism that ultimately determines the physical characteristics of that organism.

glucose a simple sugar with the chemical formula $C_6H_{12}O_6$; it is the initial product of photosynthesis. Glucose is very common in animal and plant bodies, and is a major source of energy for living organisms.

gymnosperms the name we give to seed plants that do not form flowers. These plants were present on Earth before the flowering seed plants. Representatives of this group include pines, spruce, and cypresses.

habitat the part of the environment where an organism normally lives; a habitat provides food, water, shelter, and space for an organism.

heart a four-chambered muscular organ that pumps blood received from the veins into the arteries and through the lungs to maintain the flow of blood through the circulatory system.

hemoglobin a substance in red blood cells that contains iron and is able to attract and bond with oxygen and carbon dioxide; it is the oxygen- and carbon dioxide-carrying molecule of blood.

herbivore (primary consumer) an animal that feeds primarily on plants; because an herbivore occupies the trophic level immediately above plants, it is known as the primary or first-order consumer.

heterotroph an organism (such as an animal) that cannot synthesize its own food and is dependent on consuming organic matter by eating other organisms (either plants or other animals).

heterozygous a condition where one gene (allele) of a pair is different from the other.

homeostasis the ability of a living organism to maintain an internal equilibrium by adjusting its metabolic reactions.

homozygous a condition where both genes (alleles) of a pair are the same.

hyphae a thread-like filament that forms the mycelium of fungi.

inanimate refers to a nonliving thing; inanimate objects do not have the qualities of life.

inorganic matter that is not composed of organic compounds; examples would be elements such as calcium, nitrogen, and oxygen or compounds such as salt. Water is also inorganic.

invertebrate an organism that lacks a backbone or spinal column; examples are insects, crayfish, lobsters, clams, sponge, jellyfish, and sea stars.

ion an atom that has acquired an electric charge by gaining one or more electrons (resulting in a negative charge) or losing one or more electrons (resulting in a positive charge).

ionic bond a chemical bond between two ions with opposite charges; most salts such as sodium chloride contain ionic bonds.

kidneys a pair of organs in the urinary system that filter wastes from blood while retaining necessary nutrients and water; the liquid formed by the kidneys is called urine.

Kingdom in the Linnean classification scheme, the highest category into which organisms are grouped; the five Kingdoms often used are animal, plant, fungus, protist, and monera (bacteria).

larynx the part of the respiratory system between the pharynx (the top of the throat) and the trachea (the tube leading to the lungs) that contains the vocal cords.

left atrium one of the four chambers of the heart; it receives oxygenated blood from the lungs via the pulmonary vein.

left ventricle one of the four chambers of the heart; it receives oxygenated blood from the left atrium and then pushes it out through the aorta to the rest of the body.

ligaments tough, fibrous connective tissue that connects bones together at a joint.

lung a spongy, sac-like organ that contains the alveoli where gas exchange takes place; it is part of the respiratory system.

lipid an organic molecule that is insoluble in water and feels oily. Examples are fats, oils, waxes, and triglycerides.

mammal a warm-blooded vertebrate animal with a covering of hair on the skin and milk-producing glands; humans are mammals.

marrow fatty, vascular tissue in animals that fills up many of the interior cavities of bones and is the source of red blood cells and many of the white blood cells.

metabolism all the biochemical processes that occur within a living thing that are necessary for the maintenance of life.

microbe a very small organism that cannot be seen with the unaided eye and requires the use of a microscope or at least a magnifying lens. We can also detect microorganisms by chemical tests; these living beings are everywhere, even in extreme environments such as very hot springs, very cold and dry areas, and even deep in the ocean under tremendous pressure. Some of these organisms cause diseases in animals, plants, and humans; however, most are beneficial to us and the Earth's ecosystems. In fact, we are utterly dependent upon microbes for our quality of life.

microorganism *see* microbe.

molecules the smallest unit of a substance that still has the same chemical and physical properties of the substance and is composed of two or more atoms; this can be a group of similar or different atoms held together.

Monera Kingdom this is the Kingdom that contains bacteria; all these organisms are single celled and do not contain a nucleus.

morula a spherical ball of embryonic cells that comes before the blastula.

muscular system the system of organs responsible for movement, it consists of skeletal, cardiac, and smooth muscle tissue.

mycelium a large mass of interconnected, branching hyphae is called the mycelium and constitutes the main body of the multicellular fungi. However, the mycelium is usually not seen because it is hidden throughout the food source being consumed.

myosin a protein in muscles that works in conjunction with actin to produce muscle contraction.

natural selection the process by which organisms best adapted to their environment will tend to survive and reproduce, while those less adapted will not survive or will not reproduce. This results in a new species; this contrasts with artificial selection.

nephrons tiny filtering units found in the kidney that remove wastes from the blood, but preserve water and other valuable substances. They are responsible for the production of urine.

neurotransmitter a chemical substance released at the end of a nerve axon that crosses the gap (the synapse) between itself and the dendrite end of the next nerve cell. Upon arrival at the dendrite, it will either excite or inhibit the nerve cell.

nervous system the organ system that regulates the body's responses to internal and external stimuli. In vertebrate animals, it includes the brain, spinal cord, nerves, and sense organs; the basic cell of the nervous system is the neuron.

neuron a cell of the nervous system that conducts electrical impulses.

neutron an electrically neutral subatomic particle that exists in the nucleus along with protons; it has a mass that, when combined with the mass of any protons also in the nucleus, results in almost the entire mass of the atom (electrons are very small in mass).

nucleic acid an organic molecule found in all living cells and viruses; nucleic acids in the form of molecules called deoxyribonucleic acid (DNA) and ribonucleic acid (RNA) control cellular functions and heredity.

nucleotide the molecule that is linked together to form the DNA or RNA polymer; it consists of a sugar (ribose or deoxyribose), a phosphate, and a base molecule (guanine, cytosine, thymine, adenine, or uracil).

organic matter that is related to or derived from living organisms; matter from living organisms that contains carbon.

oxygen a colorless, odorless gas that makes up about 21% of the atmosphere; it is produced by plants during photosynthesis and is used by most living organisms in respiration and metabolism of organic matter.

parasympathetic division a division of the autonomic nervous system, it is responsible for the rest and digest response by slowing the body down.

peripheral nervous system consists of nerves that connect the central nervous system to the rest of the body; it connects the brain and spinal cord to all parts of the body, including sensory nerves that bring information to the central nervous system and motor nerves that carry signals away from the brain and to the muscles, glands, or organs.

peristalsis wave-like contractions of smooth muscle in the digestive system that move food along.

pharynx the upper throat and nasal cavities; leads into the larynx.

phenotype the observable physical or biochemical characteristic of an organism as determined by its genetic makeup and environmental influences.

phloem plant tissue that has small tubes that transport food between the leaves and the roots; it is found in vascular plants only (seed and nonseed varieties).

photosynthesis the biochemical process in green plants and certain other organisms (some bacteria and protists) during which organic matter is synthesized from carbon dioxide and water using light as an energy source; oxygen is released as a byproduct.

Plant Kingdom organisms in this Kingdom are multicellular and use chlorophyll in specialized cellular structures called chloroplasts to capture sunlight energy and convert it into organic matter.

plasma a pale yellow fluid that contains proteins, blood cells, and platelets; it is the fluid portion of blood.

platelets a tiny cellular fragment that is critical in the blood-clotting process.

predator an organism that lives by preying on other organisms; the term is used most often to describe carnivores in food chains and food webs.

prey an animal hunted or caught for food; the term is used most often to describe herbivores or lower trophic-level consumers in food chains and food webs.

primary producers a photosynthetic organism such as a green plant that exists at the first trophic level in a food chain; an autotrophic organism.

proteins a group of complex organic molecules that contains carbon, hydrogen, oxygen, nitrogen, and usually sulfur and are composed of one or more chains of amino acids. Proteins are fundamental components of all living cells and include many substances, such as enzymes, hormones, and antibodies, that are necessary for the proper functioning of an organism.

Protist Kingdom this Kingdom includes single-celled organisms that contain a nucleus as part of their structure. Some are autotrophs and some are heterotrophs.

protons a positively charged subatomic particle found in the nucleus. It has mass, and the number of protons indicates the atomic number of an element and its position on the periodic table of elements.

protoplasm a semifluid, semigel substance that makes up the living matter of organisms; it is found inside the cell membrane and contains the floating organelles.

pulmonary artery an artery that carries nonoxygenated blood from the right ventricle of the heart to the lungs; this is the only artery that carries nonoxygenated blood, but because it is an artery, it carries blood away from the heart like all other arteries.

pulmonary veins a vein that carries oxygenated blood from the lungs to the left atrium of the heart; this is the only vein that carries oxygenated blood, but because it is a vein, it carries blood toward the heart like all other veins.

recessive designates a gene (allele) that does not produce a physical effect (an effect that will not appear as part of the phenotype) when present with a dominant gene (allele). It is expressed as part of the phenotype when it is present in the homozygous state (two copies of the recessive allele are present without a dominant allele also present).

red blood cells the cells in the bloodstream that have hemoglobin and carry oxygen to the body cells and carbon dioxide to the lungs; mature red blood cells do not have a nucleus.

renal system the organ system that includes the kidneys, ureters, urinary bladder, and urethra; it is responsible for filtering wastes from blood and then excreting these wastes in the form of urine. It is also called the urinary system.

reptile an organism that is a cold-blooded, usually egg-laying vertebrate of the class Reptilia. Examples are snakes, lizards, crocodiles, turtles, or dinosaurs. These organisms have an external covering of scales or horny plates and breathe with lungs.

respiration the act of inhaling and exhaling, or breathing. It can also refer to the process occurring within living cells where the energy in the chemical bonds of food is released in a series of steps that are made more efficient when the consumption of oxygen is involved. It is also known as cellular respiration and aerobic respiration when oxygen is involved or anaerobic respiration when done in the absence of oxygen.

respiratory system the body system consisting of the lungs, trachea, bronchi, bronchioles, and alveoli. It is designed for the inhalation of air and the exchange of bodily gases with that air that results in oxygenated blood. It works closely with the cardiac system so that oxygenated blood can then be distributed throughout the body.

ribonucleic acid (RNA) a polymer existing in all living cells. It is used to translate the genetic information contained in DNA into proteins.

right atrium one of the four chambers of the heart that receives nonoxygenated blood from the body through the vena cava.

right ventricle one of the four chambers of the heart that receives nonoxygenated blood from the right atrium and then pumps it to the lungs for oxygenation through the pulmonary artery.

RNA an abbreviation for ribonucleic acid.

seeded vascular plants plants that have become dominant on the earth today because they have developed pollen and seeds as adaptations.

seedless vascular plants these include club mosses, horsetails, and ferns; these plants must be in moist environments because they need water to reproduce.

sexual reproduction reproduction that involves the union of gametes from the male (sperm) and the female (egg cells).

skeletal (or striated) muscle muscle tissue that is consciously controlled by the central nervous system; this type of muscle is attached to the bones, and when it contracts, it moves the bones. This muscle is the one that forms the visible muscles and much of the mass of the body.

skeletal system the organ system that consists of bones, cartilage, and joints; supports and protects the body; produces red blood cells in the marrow of bones; and stores and releases minerals.

smooth muscle a type of muscle tissue that is usually not under conscious control; this type is usually found in the internal organs (especially the intestinal tract and in the walls of blood vessels).

sperm the male gamete.

spinal cord a cord of nerves that extends from the lower brain stem through the spinal column (vertebral column) and from which the spinal nerves branch off to various parts of the body.

sporophyte the spore-producing phase of a plant during the alternation of generations.

stomata tiny pores in the surface of a leaf or stem through which gases and water vapor pass.

sugar a compound that is water soluble, is crystalline, and belongs to the larger classification known as carbohydrates; examples are sucrose and glucose. It has a sweet taste.

sympathetic division a division of the autonomic nervous system, it is responsible for the fight or flight response by preparing the body for high energy, stressful situations.

synapse the gap across which a nerve signal passes from an axon terminal to a dendrite of another neuron or to a muscle cell or a gland; the signal is transmitted as a chemical message using a neurotransmitter molecule.

tendon tough, fibrous connective tissue that connects a muscle to a bone.

trachea a tube that is part of the respiratory system; it leads from the larynx to the bronchi and carries air toward the lungs. It is also called the windpipe.

tracheophytes trachea refers to "tube," and these vascular plants have tubes (vessels) that provide support and a means of transporting water and nutrients throughout the plant's body. Vascular plants can thus grow very tall, up to hundreds of feet. This group is further broken down into two types, the seedless vascular plants and the seeded vascular plants.

trophic (or feeding) level a group of organisms that occupy the same position in a food chain or food web; the level at which an organism exists in a food chain. Lower trophic levels are preyed upon by higher trophic levels. Plants occupy the first trophic level and are also known as producers, herbivores occupy the second trophic level and are known as primary consumers, and carnivores occupy the various levels above the herbivores and are known as primary, secondary, or tertiary consumers depending upon how many food chain links are below them.

ureter a tube that leads from a kidney to the urinary bladder; one ureter exists for each kidney. It transports urine from the kidneys to storage in the urinary bladder.

urethra a tube that leads from the urinary bladder to the outside of the body; it is used to excrete urine.

urinary bladder a sac-like organ that receives urine from the kidneys; as it fills, a signal to excrete urine is recognized by the brain, and the urge to void urine is felt.

urinary system *see* renal system.

urine   the water-based liquid produced by the kidneys that contains nitrogen wastes from cellular metabolism as well as some salts and other wastes or harmful substances. It is excreted from the body through the urinary system.

vena cava   a large vein (there are two) that carries blood to the heart from the upper body and the lower body; they empty into the right atrium of the heart.

vertebrates   animals that have a backbone or spinal column. These include mammals, fish, birds, reptiles, and amphibians.

villus   a tiny, finger-like projection inside the small intestine; the thousands of villi present in the small intestine greatly increase the surface area available for nutrient absorption; its plural is villi.

venules   a small vein, usually joined to capillaries.

white blood cells   various types of blood cells (except for the red blood cells) that have a nucleus. They are used by the body as part of the immune system to protect itself from disease and infection.

xylem   plant tissue that supports and transports water from the roots to the leaves; it is found in vascular plants only (seed and nonseed varieties).

NOTES

NOTES

NOTES

NOTES

NOTES

NOTES

NOTES

NOTES